CONTENTS

CW00742057

(Continued above right)

INTRODUCTION

Before the pub began . (1611-1899)

This account of the Linton Holme and environs are compiled here in a diary format for ease of compilation and understanding.. The purpose is to celebrate the centenary of the Linton Holme Hotel. Source material has been organised in chronological order to give an insight into the history and development of the area. Original newspaper articles and documents, combined with the recollections of some of the *older* customers of the Linton Holme Inn, have been used to describe events which have affected the community of this southern district of the City of Carlisle.

The book deals with the early origins of the place names, the development of industry in the area, the arrival of the railway, the consequent need for housing, the rise of the *corner shop*, the beginnings of the Allotment Society and much more besides. I realise that I have only *scraped the surface*, but I hope this presentation will inspire others to delve deeper.

"He lives twice who also enjoys the past"

The Linton Holme Hotel (1899-1999)

Martial (Marcus Valerius Martialis) Ca AD 40 -104

The section on the hotel includes the newspaper reports of the opposition to the building of the establishment as well as newspaper articles depicting the history of the Central Control Board for Liquor traffic and the Carlisle and District State Management Scheme (1916-1973), under which the hotel operated. The further development of the area during the 20th Century (1900-1960s) is included, with contributions from the recollections of some of the older customers of *The Lint;* as the hotel has become affectionately known.

The Origins of Linton Holme.

Today the area known as Linton Holme lies between Greystone Road and The River Petteril. This was not always so, for originally Linton Holme lay on the Botcherby (east) side of the river. It was in 1961 when work was undertaken to alter the course of the River Petteril to alleviate the flooding of the area that Linton Holme switched sides. For this reason the area is not shown on the Carlisle Socage plan of 1610.

The walls of the city were demolished in 1811, but the suburbs were not included within the city boundaries until 1887. In 1912 the city boundaries were again extended to include the medieval villages, such as Botcherby, which by this time had become indistinguishable from the expanding suburbs.

Willows still grow on The Linton Holme today.

The name Linton Holm is an appropriate one for the area :-

Linton being taken from the earlier word of *Lintern* meaning Long.

Holme is a flat piece of ground by a river, submerged in time of flood.

Throughout this book we will encounter the recurring problem of flooding in the area.

During prehistoric times and up to the arrival of the Romans it would have been largely a wooded area with willow trees thriving on the wetter lands.

Roman Cemetery on London Road.

"The strip of land on each side of London Road, Carlisle, the main road leaving the city to the south, has long been considered to have been the site of Luguvalium, and one where burials, both by cremation and inhumation, were reported to have taken place as late as the fifth century. The local press has reported finds since 1786, whenever repairs were made to the turnpike road. ....." T Patten, M.B.E. 1974

There have been many Roman artefacts unearthed in the Linton Holme area, some of which can be seen at Tullie House Museum.

For example six large flanged tiles 18 by 12 inches and 1 inch thick were found in 1894 in Brook Street, Carlisle within the area of the Roman Cemetery extending to Gallows or Harraby Hill. They were placed over a coffin, presumably of Roman date.

Earlier in 1864, Grey Street, Botchergate was the site of a find of a *"Rude Sarcophagus."* This consisted of large blocks of red sandstone each 21 inches by 25 inches forming a stone vault.

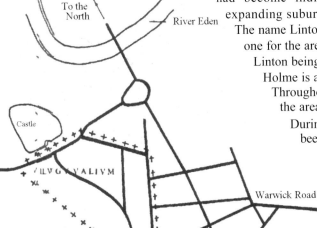

Sketch map of Carlisle showing the sites of Roman burial discoveries.

The dashed lines (- - - -) indicate the bounds of the Roman cemetary.

Inside the vault the bones of the deceased were contained within a square glass vessel, which had a letter M inside a circle, stamped on its base.

The Socage* Manor of Carlisle Castle, 1610

*Socage - A feudal tenure of land involving payment of rent or other non-military services to a superior . *Oxford Dictionary.*

Below: This Roman milestone, found in the bed of the River Petteril below Gallows Hill in 1894 proves that London Road was the Roman road south out of Luguvallium. A stone of this size could not be moved far from its original position. on Gallows Hill.

The stone has been inscribed at three different times. The text at the centre of the stone, probably the original text, has been chiselled away.

Presumably when the need came to re-inscribe the milestone it was dug up and re-positioned upside down.

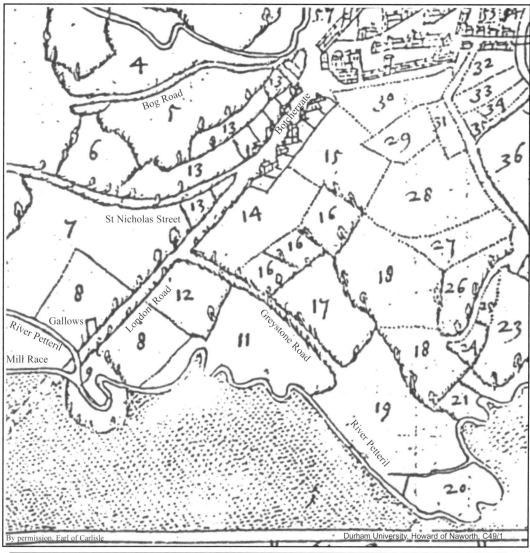

By permission, Earl of Carlisle   Durham University, Howard of Naworth, C49/1

Detail from the Socage Manor Map of Carlisle Castle, dated 1610

The red sandstone fragment below shows a head, which is half-lifesize with part of a canopy above. It was found in Charles Street in 1878. This tombstone fragment, found in the London Road area of Carlisle, gives further proof of the existence of a graveyard.

Key to relevant areas

	Acres	Roods		Acres	Roods
7. Almerye Holme	42	1	19. Bunting meadows	14	3
8. Gallows Hill	30	2	20. The Greeves meadow	8	-
9. Spittle crooke	11	1	21. Morlands	3	-
10. Paradice	18	-	22. Holemeade	5	2
11. The Maines & Graistonflat	22	2	23. Leagerd Hill	12	3
12. Seven acres	13	1	24. Sewell close	3	2
13. Spittle closes	19	-	25. Gunner close	3	-
14. Botchergate closes	15	-	26. Seven acre close	9	3
15. Aglianbye lands	14	2	27. The oxpasture	8	3
16. Wetlands	14	-	28. Twenty acre Hill	23	-
17. Fewis Hill	17	1	29. Six acre close	7	-
18. Broadmeads	33	1			

The Origins of the Environs to the Linton Holme

The tradition of the great number of hostelries on Botchergate dates back to the 1561 Dormant book of Bylaws, which stated that no Scots man or woman may walk within this city after the curfew had rung. The bell was rung at dusk and the gates to the city were closed. Any travellers locked out would need overnight accommodation along the approach roads of Botchergate, Caldewgate and Rickergate. Botchergate continued along to the old Roman road leading south out of the city (London Road).

Fewishill (no. 17. Carlisle Socage map of 1610) was the site of an earthen fortification for the parliamentary forces during the siege of Carlisle in 1644 . Today the area is known as Fusehill.

The Mains and Graiston Flat (no. 11. Carlisle Socage Manor map of 1610) The Maines being an abbreviation of "the Desmaines of the Castle and land belonging.." Today the area of Greystone derives the name from the old Graiston .

Botcherby or Botchardby (The first element 'Botchard' being of Norman French origin and the second, 'by,' Danish from an earlier settlement.) was also the site of an earthen fortification during the siege of 1644. Botchardby later became a small township of several house, pleasantly situated one mile east from Carlisle.

Botchergate or 'Botchardgate,' was a township forming the southern suburb to the City of Carlisle, containing 370 acres. The Manor Of Botchergate, or Prior Lordship, formerly belonging to the priory of Carlisle, and now to the Dean and Chapter extends over the chief part of Saint Cuthberts parish. This Township, and the hamlet of Botchardby were anciently held by one Botchard, a native of Flanders, and passed in marriage with his daughter, Isolda, to Guy, the Forester, who paid 6s. 2d. cornage for them to Henry 1, and took the name of Botchardby, which after four generations became extinct in female issue, and the estates passed to the Parvings, the Stapletones, the Musgraves, and others.
Carlisle Directory 1837 p.169

Seven Acres (no. 12. Carlisle and Socage Manor plan of 1610) was arable meadow or pasture ground lying next to the River Petteril and was part of the Socage of the Duke of Devonshire. Later we will see this area become the housing development in the fields lying next to Brook Street, off Thompson St, Alexander St, Lindisfarne St, Oswald St and Linton St.

Botchardgate Closes (Botchergate) became one of the first suburbs, with the major highway of the time running through it, on either side were poor houses of clay or wood and thatch, it was destroyed many times in raids across the border, but quickly rebuilt once danger had past.
Greystone Urban Trail.

.........Of local stone coffins there are several of interest. In 1829, when a new bridge was being made across the Petteril near Harraby Hill, a deep cutting was made on the east side of Gallows Hill, as it was locally called, and in the course of the excavations a leaden coffin was discovered. The leaden coffin was broken by its weight into three or four pieces. The contents were lost in the fall, and no vestige remained but a small part of a skull and some hair of a reddish colour
......Transactions of the Cumberland and Westmorland Antiquarian and Archaeological Society - Vol. vi p 292 NS

For many decades land lying outside the City Walls was used as refuse tips. As the City spread these tips moved further out into the outlying areas. We know that parts of Linton Holme and environs were used as tips, due to the findings unearthed when any building work has taken place. It was also thought of as a good way to provide better drainage for the low lying areas prone to flooding. The tips would be raked over and re-used, in this way raising the level of the land.

Early Land Ownership.

The Duke of Devonshire P.C. is Lord of the manor of the Socage of Carlisle Castle.
The Dean and Chapter are lords of the Manor of Botchergate.
These with the Earl of Lonsdale are chief Landowners.
The land is principally in pasture but some oats are grown .The soil is clay and loam; the subsoil is marl.
The Cumberland Directory 1910 .

Botcherby Corn Mill & Farm (1644-1995)

Botcherby Mill stood in Greystone Road where the housing estate of Riverside Way now stands, but the mill race has been filled. The Site is medieval and a mill which stood there in 1644 was destroyed in the Siege of Carlisle. Its replacement was swept away by floods (along with some cattle) in November 1771.

In 1790 the Mill was restored by Margery Jackson (1722 -1812), also known as 'The Carlisle Miser.' The Mill was an old family property which she had inherited from her grandfather; Thomas Jackson.
The Corn Mill brought in an annual rent of £7 and above the front door to the Mill was a tablet which read :
"Miss Margery Jackson, sister of W.N.Jackson Esq., rebuilt this mill in 1790"
 "There was a footpath leading from The Head of Botchergate (Midland Bank) to Botcherby, it was used by the poor working men to walk to Botcherby Cornmill to have their *'peck of meal'* ground for their families."
Margery Jackson (1722 -1812) Life and times of the Carlisle Miser. H.R.Hallaway.

Painting of Botcherby Mill by J J Hodgson circa 1900

No. 10 Restaurant

Botcherby Corn Mill was served by a mill race from the River Petteril, this mill race was also the source of water for the Raven Nook mill of 1850.

On Margery Jackson's death.......... "On the Monday 10th. inst. at Botcherby, near this City, at the advanced age of ninety, Miss MARGERY JACKSON, a maiden lady, who was for many years an inhabitant of Carlisle...........Though in possession of a fortune of more than £50,000, her annual expenditure,.............. certainly amounted to very little....... If she seldom or never sacrificed to the pleasures of the table, the more seductive attractions of the bottle held her regard. Her usual beverage was brandy mixed with wine.......To say that our heroine never did a generous action, would be an injustice to her memory..... The character of this extraordinary woman may furnish to all our readers a lesson, in teaching us that wealth ought to be valued as a means of doing good.
The bulk of her property, with the exception of some small legacies, Miss Jackson has bequeathed to Mr Joseph Bowman of Botcherby."   Extracts from Margery's obituary, *Carlisle Journal,* 15 February 1812

Joseph Bowman was a Quaker, he lived two miles from Carlisle in the country village of Botcherby, with his sister Mary and Robert their blind brother. They lived in a large house with an orchard on Wood Street, Botcherby; his house still stands today, but most of the orchard has been built upon. The circumstances of Joseph's acquisition were questionable and although he lived to 81 years old he was never secure in his inheritance (For further details see H.R. Hallaway's book on Margery Jackson). Joseph died in 1848 in possession of Margery's fortune, on his death he left all his worldly goods to two friends. The principal legatee being a John Norman, who had already changed his surname to Bowman, in compliance with Joseph's wishes, when he heard the will was being contested, due to the fact that on Joseph's death the secret of the dubious way in which he had received his inheritance from Margery was made public.
Some of Margery's property went to a Charles James Graham of Anns Hill but most of it did go to John Norman (now John Bowman), his children and his children's children to the fourth and fifth genera-tions.   *Margery Jackson, Life and Times of the Carlisle Miser.* H R Hallaway.

Margery Jackson, who owned Botcherby Mill at one time (from an etching by James MacMillan)

1848   The Heirs of John Bowman Esq.
Extracts from the last will and testament of John Bowman, a gentleman of Botcherby in the Parish of St.Cuthberts Carlisle, showing how his lands around the Linton Holme were distributed .
"........... to my grand daughters Ann Hodgson and Mary Robinson and their respective heir .... all my mill ...... called Botcherby Mill with the houses, outhouses and Lands lying near there in the Townfields or Townships of Botcherby, Botchergate .... in the Parish of St. Cuthberts and called Lowfield Meadow .... (and) two Closes called Fewishill. .... I give bond devise to my grandson John Norman of Carlisle and his heirs .... all those my houses, outhouses, yards and gardens at or near Botcherby .... also all those Closes or enclosures on or near Botcherby aforesaid called .... (and) two Linton Holme Closes."   *Cumbria Heritage Services, Records Office, Carlisle.*
The painting at the top of the page is by J J Hodgson, who is probably a relative of Ann Hodgson who inherited the mill from John Bowman (see above). It is interesting to compare the painting with the photographs of the mill over the page. The mill race ran along the back of the mill parallel to Greystone Road. This agrees with the marks from the water wheel on the wall at the back of the mill; shown in a photograph over the page.

Botcherby Corn Mill & Farm (1644-1995)

1864 Additions to Botcherby Mill were built for John Norman to a design by J. Hodgson. See right.

1910 Thomas Johnston was the cow keeper at Botcherby Mill farm .

1925 John Johnston had taken over as the cow keeper at the farm .

1928 John Dixon recalls as a boy of 14 years old he worked on Casey's Farm, Wood Street, Botcherby. He was paid £2. 10s. a week, with 10s. being deducted for his keep. He was expected to sleep at the farm, but his room had no ceiling,

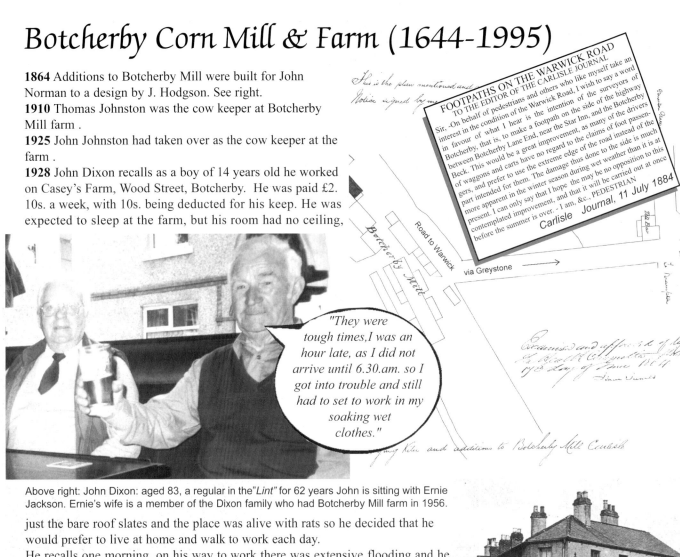

FOOTPATHS ON THE WARWICK ROAD
TO THE EDITOR OF THE CARLISLE JOURNAL

Sir, -On behalf of pedestrians and others who like myself take an interest in the condition of the Warwick Road, I wish to say a word in favour of what I hear is the intention of the surveyors of Botcherby, that is, to make a footpath on the side of the highway between Botcherby Lane End, near the Star Inn, and the Botcherby Beck. This would be a great improvement, as many of the drivers of waggons and carts have no regard to the claims of foot passengers, and prefer to use the extreme edge of the road instead of the part intended for them. The damage thus done to the side is much more apparent in the winter season during wet weather than it is at present. I can only say that I hope the may be no opposition to this contemplated improvement, and that it will be carried out at once before the summer is over. - I am, &c., PEDESTRIAN

Carlisle Journal, 11 July 1884

> "They were tough times, I was an hour late, as I did not arrive until 6.30.am. so I got into trouble and still had to set to work in my soaking wet clothes."

Above right: John Dixon: aged 83, a regular in the"*Lint*" for 62 years John is sitting with Ernie Jackson. Ernie's wife is a member of the Dixon family who had Botcherby Mill farm in 1956.

just the bare roof slates and the place was alive with rats so he decided that he would prefer to live at home and walk to work each day.

He recalls one morning, on his way to work there was extensive flooding and he could not see the footpath across Melbourne Park, so he walked further up Greystone Road to cross at Botcherby Mill Farm, but as the mill and the farm were so low set he had to wade through chest high water to reach the farm. *"They were tough times, I was an hour late, as I did not arrive until 6.30.am. so I got into trouble and still had to set to work in my soaking wet clothes."* He also recalls going to the Star Inn with a tin to be filled up with beer for the farm workers to drink on a dinnertime.

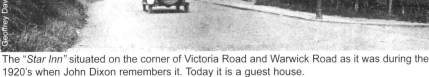

The "*Star Inn*" situated on the corner of Victoria Road and Warwick Road as it was during the 1920's when John Dixon remembers it. Today it is a guest house.

1934 Burtonwood Motor Engineering Co. Ltd. were now established at Botcherby Mill.

1952 The Cumberland Tyre Co. were now in business at the mill. The photograph (right) shows the back of the mill where marks made by the waterwheel can be seen on the wall to the right of the door. An enlarged view of that section of wall can be seen at the top left of the adjacent page.

1955 Botcherby Mill had existing buildings altered to accommodate large vehicles for Mr Mandale.

THE REMOULDING SPECIALISTS
CUMBERLAND TYRE Co. Ltd.
BOTCHERBY MILL
GREYSTONE ROAD
CARLISLE
Tel: 1566
New Tyre Supplies
Giant Tyre Specialists
The Complete Tyre Retreading Service

Carlisle Directory 1952

Detail of the mill photograph on the previous page showing the score marks made on the wall by the rotation of the waterwheel.

Right: On **Friday 31 August 1956** the River Petteril, no longer peaceful and tranquil but swollen and foaming, threatened to flood houses in the Greystone Road area after overnight torrential rain.

Right: Mrs Sarah Dixon and Mrs J Nanson wade through the waters, which flooded their yard at Botcherby Mill Farm, Greystone Road, Carlisle, to reach dry land. The water was running through the house and flooded all the ground floor ....Botcherby Mill Farm was the worst affected house in Carlisle ......

1959 A car wash was installed at Botcherby Mill by Mr Mandale.

11 April, 1962 Mr Mandale appealed against Carlisle City Council's refusal to allow his firm (J W Hodgson (Transport) Ltd.) to continue the development of the land as a transport centre.

Left: Greystone Road was flooded again in **March 1968**, causing a bullock to come in from the fields.

1979 Botcherby Mill had now become a motorists' discount shop (see below).

1995 The now derelict building burnt down (see right).

Botcherby Mill land an "eyesore"

PEOPLE in Warwick Road, Greystone Road and Waller Street claimed at a public inquiry in Carlisle Town Hall yesterday that broken-down lorries, dead sheep and oil drums were making Botcherby Mill land into an eyesore.

Mr Bernard Mandale, Grey-

1995 The remains of Botcherby Mill were demolished to make way for the housing development of Riverside Way.

7

The Carlisle Old Charity School which had it's links with Bowmans Close. (1717-1851)

In July 1717, a charity school was established in Carlisle by voluntary subscriptions for teaching poor children to read, and instructing them in the Christian religion and such other things as should be suitable to their condition. Records do not show the exact location of The Old Charity School, but they do tell us that certain fields owned by the Dean and Chapter were let to tenants whose rents went towards supporting the school. One such area was Bowmans Closes; today the area of Bowman Street.

3 May 1717

A Mr Richard Wilkinson was unanimously chosen as master of the school.

A Mr Raylton was to seek out for a proper room for a school before midsummer next.

23 July 1717

A letter from John Walton, secretary of trustees of the Charity school to the Rev. Todd Vice Dean of the Cathedral ....ordered that the humble thanks of the trustees be given to the Rev. Todd, Vice Dean for the sermon preached by him in the Cathedral Church of 21st. July 1717 upon the opening of the said Charity School.

In **1732** the sum of £20 was laid out for the purchase of Hill Houses Estate, 15 miles from Carlisle. The rent brought in by this estate went to support the Charity School.

In 1783 Hill Houses Estate was sold and in **1785** other property was purchased by the trustees of the Charity School.

... Land lying half a mile from the City of Carlisle, two Closes called Beaumonts Closes, (BOWMANS CLOSES).

In the parish of St Cuthberts, Carlisle, containing four acres, more or less, held in the Socage of Carlisle Castle, at the customary rent of 10s .....

19 June 1717

The trustees were to meet at the schoolhouse on Michaelmas day.

Several donations and legacies were given to the school soon after its establishment.

20 February 1718

Nicholas Robinson bequeathed the sum of £40 for the education of poor children in Carlisle ...

28 February 1718

Samuel How bequeathed to the Mayor of Carlisle, four senior aldermen of Carlisle and the Dean and Chapter the sum of £320 to be put out at interest on good security. The interest of £200 thereof to be employed and laid out for and towards the support of the Charity School.

The Charity Commissioners Report of 1821 refers to *'The Girls Charity School'* and how the charity income was distributed after the school had been closed. It also states: *'There was no school-room belonging to the charity.'* This is probably the reason why it has not been possible to determine the school's location.

This rent brought in from Bowmans Closes was for the use and benefit of The Charity School. The original plan of the institution appears from the books to have been for the education of boys, the first resolution entered being one for the *"maintenance in clothing and education for 10 boys".*

Subsequently girls were admitted and latterly girls only. Twenty or twenty one girls were educated and clothed by the money raised in rents paid on Bowmans Closes, and by aid of subscription up to **May 1817**; at this time the Central School was established and an annual sum of £20 out of the income of the Charity School was given to the Central School.

Below: On the **22 August 1884** this advertisement appeared in the *Carlisle Journal* for the sale of Bowman's Close as building land.

VALUABLE BUILDING LAND IN CARLISLE FOR SALE.

THE TRUSTEES of HOWE'S CHARITY are prepared to accept OFFERS for the SALE, by PRIVATE CONTRACT, in ONE LOT, of a Large and Valuable Plot of BUILDING LAND, known as BOWMAN'S CLOSE, situate in the Parish of Saint Mary, in the City of CARLISLE, and containing 5a. 2r. 13p. or 27,013 square yards. The Land which is only a short distance from the London Road, is bounded by Brook Street, Edward Street, Grey Street, and Fusehill Street, and lies in the heart of an extensive district, which is rapidly becoming covered with Buildings.

Offers can be sent in up to the 30th September next, either to Messrs. SAUL, Solicitors, Castle Street, or Messrs. NANSON, Solicitors, Fisher Street, Carlisle, from whom further particulars can be obtained, and at whose offices a Plan of the Property can be seen.

Left: detail from the subscription role of the Charity School which shows that Joseph Wilson provided a schoolhouse free of charge to the charity.

The Mains (The Albion Works)
now Bendalls Sheet Metal Works, London Road.

The Mains on the Socage Map of 1610 was so called because it was part of the Desmaine of Carlisle Castle.

The original factory appears to have been built on this site adjacent to the house called 'The Mains' in **1799**. At this time one Edward Rothwell gave up the lease he held on a cotton mill at English Damside. At about the same time John Forster of *'Harraby House,'* left his fulling mill at Harraby Green. A report in the *Carlisle Journal,* Saturday 27th June 1818 (see this page), mentions that the factory, has been in operation for 19 years. As Rothwell and Forster were part owners this fits in with 1799 being the construction date.   *Denis Perriam*

Returning to Carlisle From The South.

"..............On crossing Harraby Bridge the first object which attracts our attention is the Cotton Mill of Messrs. Rothwell & Co. called The Mains ...."*The Carlisle Guide & Directory,* 1811

27 June 1818

To show the healthiness of the employment in the Cotton Mill of Messrs. Rothwell & Co. Mains, near this City, we have authority to state that in the period of nineteen years during which these works have been carried on only one death has taken place and that was of a young woman, occasioned by her imprudence in bathing when heated. These works are the first that were heated by steam in this neighbourhood and are well ventilated.

Carlisle Journal

LONDON ROAD

Mains

·76

M.S. { Carlisle
Penrith 17

85

LP

B.M. 84·9

Background map: Cumbria Heritage Services, Record Office, Carlisle.

October 1826

In October James Losh visited Mr.Rothwell who has the management of a very large manufactory near Harraby.
This is what he had to say in his diary .. *"I was very much pleased to see the order of cleanliness of everything connected with it. The children looked healthy and some of the men with whom I talked appeared to be satisfied that their masters paid them as much as they could afford"*

Carlisle Library

The Mains (continued)

· 11 March 1835

Carlisle From East of The River Petteril   *J. W. Carmichael, 1835*
showing the Mains Cotton Mill, established by Rothwell and Co. in 1799.

Tullie House Museum

Melancholy Accident - On Saturday Last.

"A most melancholy accident occurred in the cotton mill of Messrs. Rothwell & Co, at Mains near this City, in which a girl by the name of Rachael Brown, aged fifteen years lost her life. She was engaged in attending a part of the machinery in the carding room, and near the place where she was at work is an upright shaft having a rotary motion. This is encased in tin, to within almost six inches of the top. The case is closed with wire pins which cannot be removed by hand, and so well is the joint formed that the opening in it is scarcely sufficient to admit of the insertion of a sixpence. Against the shaft, it seems the girl had been leaning (away from her work) and by some means which appear almost unaccountable a part of her dress had been drawn through the slight opening we have named, and revolving with the shaft soon drew her dress so tight about her that she was unable to cry out for assistance, She was seen almost immediately; but before the engine could be stopped her leg had got jammed between the shaft and a pillar and it was broken in two places; and she was otherwise seriously injured. She was conveyed home, and every attention paid to her that skill could suggest or humanity devise; but not withstanding every effort she gradually sunk, and died on Sunday. A coroner's inquest was held upon the body, and a verdict returned of accidental death. The parents of the deceased are poor but industrious people, with a large family, and were found in a state of great distress. We hope their case will be enquired into by the humane and charitable, and such relief afforded them as may be required."

Carlisle Journal, 6 April 1839

Obituary

"At Halfway Houses, London Road on the first instance, Mr. James Hargreaves, mechanic aged eighty two years, much respected. He was upwards of thirty years in employment of Messrs. Rothwell and Co. Mains near this City ....In early life he was considered one of the most skilled mechanics in Lancashire and some of the most eminent cotton spinners in the Kingdom bear testimony to the utility and value of his inventions."

Carlisle Journal, 9 September 1843

The cotton mill was put up for sale in October 1855 but apparently no buyer came forward and in February 1857 it was decided to erect a new building to contain power looms.

Only nine years after this improvement, the factory was advertised for sale again, now described as a power loom weaving factory.

Right: Detail from the letterhead of Brown, Tran & Co. which shows the appearance of the Albion Mills after its conversion into a power loom factory. Compare this with Carmichael's view of 1835 (shown on the opposite page), which shows a six storey building.

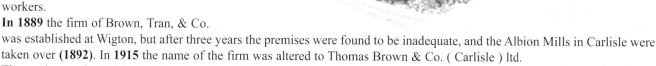

Cumbria Heritage Services, Record Office, Carlisle

Carlisle's Textile Industries, The Albion Mills, Thomas Brown & Co. ltd.

"For many years the Albion Mills in London Road have been successively occupied by Cotton manufacturers, Woollen manufacturers, and hosiery workers.

In 1889 the firm of Brown, Tran, & Co. was established at Wigton, but after three years the premises were found to be inadequate, and the Albion Mills in Carlisle were taken over **(1892)**. In **1915** the name of the firm was altered to Thomas Brown & Co. (Carlisle) ltd. The works are situated just off London Road, but few people realise what an enormous number of looms and weaving apparatus is contained in the buildings. The firm has been so successful in recent years that extensions have been made from time to time, and, as a matter of fact, workmen are at present engaged in building another large warehouse where additional producing plant will be installed...The extensions to the works have meant an increase in the number of employees, and now there are over 200 workers.
Carlisle Journal, Civic Week Supplement, **August 1928.**

November 1924 - The Albion works were purchased by the firm of Mr. James Bendall

9 December 1949 -
"25 YEARS PROGRESS, CARLISLE FIRM'S ANNIVERSARY. Last month had a special, significance for a well known Carlisle firm. It was in November 1924, a quarter of a century ago that the late Mr. James Bendall, a Dumfries man, and his two sons came to Carlisle and set up in business here as sheet metal workers and motor body repairers. Now the firm of James Bendall & Sons is known throughout the two counties and even much further afield, into Scotland and over to Newcastle. There is a staff of 85 highly skilled workmen in the Albion Works on London Road and as Mr. George Bendall told an inquiring *JOURNAL* reporter this week:- *We can just about make anything that's made with metal."*

Memo from **Brown, Tran & Co. ltd.**
FANCY FLANNEL MANUFACTURERS, CARLISLE.
ALBION MILLS, LONDON ROAD

The Mains (continued)

........A short tour through the works certainly suggested this, for there, in course of construction, was a wide variety of articles in sheet metal .... from bread tins for a local bakery to the funnels and piping associated with factory ventilation and fume extraction, stainless steel dye vats to coal-mining plant, and fire-escapers to all weather cabs for farm tractors.

Work For Export

Messrs. Bendall are responsible for sheet-metal work and maintenance, machine guards, etc., of practically all the Carlisle and district factories and works and many throughout Cumberland. They even contribute towards the export drive, for one of their varied jobs is the manufacture for packing cases of goods destined for overseas. To the motoring public, of course Bendall's is associated more particularly with repairs to the body-work of cars. It is to the Albion Works " hospital " that shattered wrecks from accidents go for treatment to emerge resplendent and dentless, with all their scars removed.

The association of the Bendall family with the motor car goes back much further than a quarter of a century, back to the days when the old coach and gig makers began to change their roles to emerge as motor body repairers.

55 Years Ago - The firm was really established in Dumfries in 1884 by the late Mr. James Bendall, farther of the present directors, and as a sheet metal works and dairy utensils makers was well known throughout South Scotland. During the first world war, staff and equipment were diverted to the manufacture of aeroplane petrol tanks, engine plates etc.

After the war, Mr. James Bendall and his sons went into partnership with a Dumfries metal working company for seven years. That partnership was dissolved when the Bendalls came to Carlisle.

Bendall's today consists mainly of large modern factory sheds. The offices however occupy part of the original mill which still survives and can be seen from London Road

Buses For the Isle of Man - Their first premises were in Warwick Road, the site of what are now the showrooms and offices of Messers. Harrisons motor engineers (no. 37 Warwick Rd.). One of their first big contracts was the panel dome backs of six Cumberland Motor Company buses destined for service in the Isle Of Man. When more extensive premises were necessary, new works were built on Duke's Road in 1929. By that time their general sheet metal work was expanding as well as the motor body repairing side of the business, and by 1939 the staff had increased to 38. The Dukes Road premises, in their turn, became too small and so the Albion Works were purchased towards the end of 1939. Before that, however, their building in Duke's Road had been the first in the City to be requisitioned - two days before the outbreak of war .

Bendall's Boast - Now the Albion Works, the well equipped workshops cover an area of 30,000 sq. ft. . Since July an adjoining building has been vacated by a box making firm, has been turned into the sheet-metal works -there are a score of gas and electric wielding plants alone - so that now a hundred cars can be accommodated in the repair shops.

The staff incorporates every trade in motor body making and repairing -trimmers, panel beaters, blacksmiths, cellulose and coach painters, etc. - so that it is Bendall's proud boast that no outside help at all is required to re-instate the worst damaged vehicle."   *Carlisle Journal,* 9 December 1949

The firm of Bendall's & Sons has come a long way since that newspaper report of the late 1940's and still carries out it's business from The Albion Works, London Road Carlisle.

1942 An interesting roadside feature which appeared at various locations around Carlisle early in 1942 can be seen on the photo (right), which shows the entrance to Bendall's on London Road. Police pillar telephone number 15 was situated on the pavement at the factory entrance.

An article in the *Carlisle Journal,* 10 February 1942, explained their operation and how they were to be used.   The boxes consisted of a a unit incorporating a standard micro - telephone for police use and a loudspeaker and transmitter for public use. This was a '*state of the art*' emergency communication for the time. The micro - telephone was only available to the police, enabling the officer to report in when on the beat. A member of the public could quickly obtain assistance at the public side of the pillar merely by pulling and holding open the door until the operator answered. On release the door was self - closing. The article described the possible uses of the boxes as follows:

"Members of the public can:

1. More conveniently and speedily request attendance and assistance of the police in case of trouble, lost property, disturbances, persons acting suspiciously, accident etc..

2. Request attendance of the Fire Brigade.

3. More easily give helpful and valuable information to the police when they suspect anyone has committed or is about to commit a crime, or that any crime is being committed."

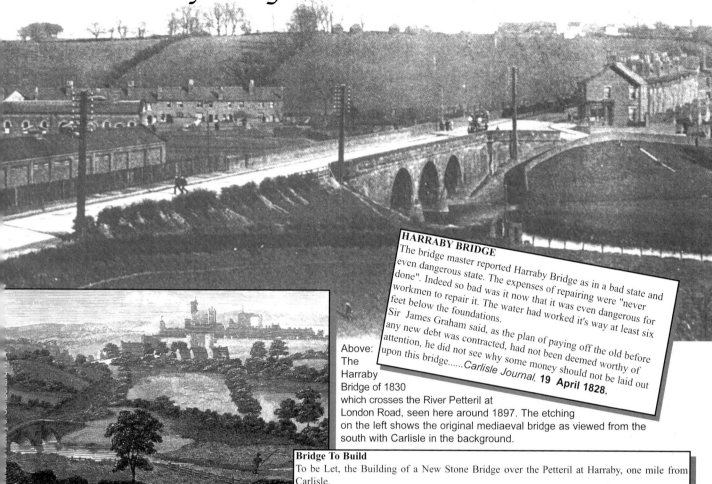

HARRABY BRIDGE

The bridge master reported Harraby Bridge as in a bad state and even dangerous state. The expenses of repairing were "never done". Indeed so bad was it now that it was even dangerous for workmen to repair it. The water had worked it's way at least six feet below the foundations.

Sir James Graham said, as the plan of paying off the old before any new debt was contracted, had not been deemed worthy of attention, he did not see why some money should not be laid out upon this bridge......*Carlisle Journal*, **19 April 1828.**

Above: The Harraby Bridge of 1830 which crosses the River Petteril at London Road, seen here around 1897. The etching on the left shows the original mediaeval bridge as viewed from the south with Carlisle in the background.

Bridge To Build

To be Let, the Building of a New Stone Bridge over the Petteril at Harraby, one mile from Carlisle.

Plans and specifications may be seen at the Clerk of the Peaces Office, Carlisle by whom tenders will be received until Saturday the 31st. day of May instant, when the contractor will be declared at the Grand Jury Room. ....*Carlisle Journal*, **17 May 1828.**

HARRABY BRIDGE. the centre arch of this old and inconvenient structure over the Petteril, at Harraby, which was about to be pulled down, fell sometime during Thursday night, or early yesterday morning. We are glad to say, without injuring any person. The water was not swollen, and no carriage of any kind was near it when the arch fell, although a few hours previous to the catastrophe, two heavily laden wagons passed over southward. Another large wagon approached after the fall, and which passed over the temporary wooden bridge, was the means of timely alarm being given before the starting of the coaches which leave Carlisle early in the morning. Persons were immediately placed to guard future passengers from danger, and proper railings to prevent accidents have since been erected at each end: The most active preparations are making for laying the foundations of a new Bridge.
Carlisle Journal, **28 February 1829.**

POLICE.................six labourers employed at the Harraby new bridge, were taken into custody by watchmen between two and three o'clock on Saturday morning for fighting and making a disturbance in English Street when in a state of intoxication. They were discharged by the Mayor on giving bail to appear when called upon .... *Carlisle Journal*, **28 March 1829.**

The Petteril Bridge (Harraby Bridge),

(in those days it had a flat and low parapet)

"this was a hazard, many a hat was lost and many an umbrella was blown inside out .At the end of the bridge, was the wicket gate with a flight of steps leading to the back way to Petteril Terrace, (and the most used) as the front road was further on up the road, and mostly used for vehicular traffic. ....Then football came to the fore............an apprentice joiner put up goal posts in the field below the bridge at Harraby Green, where the mill dam ran along side..............Petteril Bridge was a good place to watch a game, I've seen many a crowd watching a match on a Saturday afternoon. The team was called Harraby Athletic"
Our City, Our People 1889-1978　　　Memories by Mildred Edwards.

The Harraby Bridge remained in the same state until further improvements took place between **1938** and **1940**. The bridge was widened and the road was then improved at a total cost of £32,525. The widening was recorded on a marble plaque set into the bridge parapet, see below.

A Man Drowned In The Petteril

On Friday last an inquest was held at The Railway Hotel, before W. Carrick, Esq., Coroner, on view of the body of a man named William Sanderson, who was drowned in The River Petteril on the previous day. Information having been sent to The County Constabulary that a man was lying in the water, P.C.Cowman proceeded to the place and found the deceased there, about sixty yards below the bridge, near to the Mains Factory. He took the body to The Railway Hotel . In the pockets of the deceased found a tobacco box, a razor two or three working tools, and fifteen pence. There was no evidence to show how the deceased got there, or whether it was an accident or he had committed suicide. On Monday last when he went to his work the foreman noticed that he was the worse for drink and told him to go home. He left the place and was not seen again until he was found in the River on Thursday. The Jury returned a verdict of 'Found Drowned'
Carlisle Journal, **15 March 1864.**

The Railway

The Newcastle and Carlisle Railway was the first to enter Carlisle. The passenger shed was built near the Mains on London Road, about a mile from the city centre. This was because the railway was primarily a goods line and looped around the southern end of the city to the canal basin.

Passengers travelled to or from the city centre by horse-drawn omnibus; a rather tedious way to start or end a journey.

NEWCASTLE AND CARLISLE RAILWAY

To be LET, the Cutting, Embanking, and Forming of part of the line of Railway between the River PETTERIL and the Harraby and Botcherby road. -A specification and section may be seen at the office of Messers. Hodgson and Nanson, solicitors, Carlisle, where tenders must be delivered on or before Saturday the 28th. September.

Railway Office, Sept.11th. 1833.

Carlisle Journal, 21 September 1833

(1)

AN

A C T

FOR

Making and maintaining a Railway or Tramroad from the Town of *Newcastle upon Tyne*, in the County of the Town of *Newcastle upon Tyne*, to the City of *Carlisle*, in the County of *Cumberland*, with a Branch thereout.

[ROYAL ASSENT, 22d *May* 1829.]

WHEREAS the making and maintaining of a Railway or Tramroad, with proper Works and Conveniences adjoining thereto or connected therewith, for the Passage of Waggons and other Carriages from the Town of *Newcastle upon Tyne*, in the County of the Town of *Newcastle upon Tyne*, in and through the several Parishes and Places hereinafter mentioned, in the several Counties of *Newcastle upon Tyne*, *Northumberland*, *Durham*, and *Cumberland*, to the City of *Carlisle*, in the said County of *Cumberland*, with a Branch Railway or Tramroad thereout, commencing at or near a certain Place called *Elswick Dean*, in the Township of *Elswick*, in the County of *Northumberland*, and terminating at the West Side of a certain Street called *Thornton Street*, in *Newcastle upon Tyne*, will be of great Advantage to the Agricultural and Commercial Interests

[9.] A

First page of the Act of Parliament for the building of the Newcastle / Carlisle Railway.

................their present station being upward of a mile from the centre of the town, the passengers are put to very great inconvenience and much loss in consequence......*Carlisle Journal.*
*25 February, **1848***

NEWCASTLE AND CARLISLE RAILWAY.
No.   1837.
o'Clock.
From Wetheral ; to and from Carlisle on the same Day.
2nd Class—Paid 1s 0d
This Ticket must be shown to the Station Keeper at Carlisle, previous to taking your Seat on your return.
NOTICE.—No *Gratuity* allowed to be taken by any Guard, Porter, or other Servant of the Company

Copy of Original: First Ticket issued   1837
o'Clock
Date   0
2nd Class—Paid   1
No.

Coal Staiths

RAILWAY STATION

Mains Cotton Works

1836 - "The station, from whence the road opens, adjoins the London road at Gallows-hill, from whence it will be continued ultimately by a tunnel under the London road, passing the extensive cotton works of Messrs. Cowen as well as those of Messrs Slater & Co., and the stupendous works now erecting by Messrs. P. Dixon and Sons, in Shaddongate (which are likely to employ more than a thousand work-people) and so skirting the suburbs of the town, proceed to the basin of the canal."

Sketch of the Railroad from Carlisle to Greenhead, 13 July 1836
by Henry Brooke (Record Office, Carlisle D/Ing/178(6))

The Railway

In 1839 Francis Wishaw visited the Mains station and described the site as follows:-

"......the booking office is in a detached rustic building: but is inconveniently situate with respect to the passenger shed, which is on the other side of the station; foot passengers, having taken their tickets in the office, have some little way to go before boarding the carriages.......
The goods-shed is detached and is on the same side of the railway as the booking-office, and opposite to the passenger shed.....The Landsale coal depot is in the rear of, and at a little distance from the booking office and goods shed. It is of quadrangle form, having a shed on two sides and one at each end, enclosing an open space for common roadcarts, which enter and leave this depot under the end nearest the London Road, from which there is an entrance distinct from that to the passenger station.
The Railway, which communicates with this depot by means of a turntable on two sidings running parallel to and between it and the passenger station, passes in the middle of and along both sides and ends, with a turntable at each angle. Underneath each side are twenty cells for common road carts into which the coals or lime are discharged from the Railway wagons above by openings left between the rails and a proper flap in the bottom of each wagon. The Railway also communicates by short branches with the locomotive engine house and the repairing shops. The engine house will hold eight engines and tenders. The engine turntables are each of 13ft. 6 inches. diameter. The Carlisle Depot and Station occupy altogether about six acres of ground.

Francis Wishaw 1842 (1839)
The Railways of Great Britain

NEWCASTLE-UPON-TYNE & CARLISLE RAILWAY.

THE DIRECTORS HEREBY GIVE NOTICE, that MONDAY, the 18th instant, having been fixed for OPENING the LINE throughout, the Ordinary Business of the Railway will be suspended for that day, and that the Completion of the Communication between Newcastle and Carlisle, a distance of 60 Miles, will be celebrated by a Procession of Railway Trains, the arrangements for which will be as follows :—

The PROCESSION will leave the Company's Station, at Redheugh, Newcastle, at 11 o'clock in the Morning, *precisely*, (stopping on their rout at Blaydon, Stocksfield, Hexham, Haydon Bridge, Greenhead, and Milton,) for the Company's Station, at the Canal Basin, Carlisle, where it will arrive about 3 o'clock, and after giving time for refreshment at Carlisle, will leave the Company's Station at the London Road, Carlisle, precisely at 5 o'clock for Newcastle, stopping at the same places as in going. And for the accommodation of the friends of this important undertaking, and the Public resident at Carlisle and its vicinity, who may be desirous of joining the Procession at Newcastle, a Train will leave the London Road Station at 6 o'clock in the Morning for that place, calling at the various Stations above-mentioned.

Tickets for the Opening day only, may be purchased for 10s. each, at the Railway Stations; at the Close, Newcastle; London Road, Carlisle; Blaydon, Hexham, Haydon Bridge, Greenhead, and Milton.

By Order,
JOHN ADAMSON, Secretary.
Railway Office, Close, Newcastle-upon-Tyne,
5th June, 1838,

The London Road Station site as it appears today.

In these early days of steam engines it was not uncommon for boilers on engines to explode, see right.
On **1 January 1863** the passenger facilities at London Road were terminated and transferred to the Citadel Station and then, only one year later, a disastrous fire occurred at the London Road Station, see below.

SERIOUS FIRE AT THE NEWCASTLE & CARLISLE RAILWAY STATION

On Saturday night last (30th. April) a fire broke out in the Engine Shed of the Newcastle Railway Company at the London Road Station, Carlisle, and besides being destructive to a considerable amount of property, we regret to add that in one or two cases life has been endangered.

The fire was first discovered a little before 11.o.clock and the alarm having been given to the neighbourhood it was quickly communicated to the town, where the policemen sprang their rattles, and the city fire engines were at once horsed and manned and despatched with all speed to the scene of the conflagration....By the time the fire engine arrived on the spot the flames had obtained such a hold that all hope of saving the shed seemed to be gone, and the efforts officials and servants of the company, together with volunteered assistance, were directed towards saving the engines in the shed.........

A small fire engine belonging to the company, supplied with water from a plug near to the Railway Hotel, was set to work, but the efforts were to no avail, as the place was quickly gutted and unroofed.........When day dawned the remains of the engines and sheds presented a ruinous appearance. The engines, of course were stripped of all the wood about them, and instead of bright painted boilers they were all more or less bruised, rusted and blistered. The building is merely a shell, and of it the only things that remain are the broken windows in the blackened walls.........It is scarcely possible at present to estimate the damage done until the engines have been thoroughly examined, and the cause of the fire is also, as yet, a mystery.

Carlisle Journal, 3 May 1864

Shocking Accident - Explosion of Locomotive Boiler

On Wednesday morning a great alarm was created in the station yard of the Newcastle and Carlisle Railway, at London Road, near the City, by the explosion of the boiler of the Adelaide Locomotive engine. The engine had just arrived in the station yard, with a train of empty coal wagons from the Canal Basin, and having taken in a supply of coke, the engine driver, Wm. Simpson, was about to start forward when suddenly a terrific noise was heard, and the whole train became enveloped in a dense cloud of steam and smoke. On examination it was found, that, owing to some cause not yet precisely ascertained, the upper part of the fire box of the engine had burst, and that with such a tremendous force had the steam rushed forth, that it had lifted the engine bodily from the rails to a distance of eighteen inches, and striking the engine man between the legs and on the lower part of the body, had thrown him backwards a distance of several yards, and he was found at the bottom of the fourth coal wagon from the tender! The stoker, Peter Short, who was standing on top of the coke tender was thrown into the first coal wagon . When the engine-man was discovered he was insensible, and it was found that the lower part of his body was dreadfully scalded, and his head much bruised, by striking against the sides of a coal-wagon, and several contusions about the face. The stoker, though severely injured, was not dangerously so. No time was lost in having Simpson removed home and medical assistance provided. In the course of two hours he became sensible, but had no knowledge of how the accident had occurred. This (Friday) morning he is considered to be going on favourably, but cannot be pronounced out of danger. The stoker is rapidly recovering Simpson, who is a careful steady man, and well aquainted with his business, says the engine was " priming " when he passed the Dalston-Road, which is only a few hundred yards from where the explosion took place, and therefore the supply of water must have been abundant. The most likely cause of the accident, however, is deficiency of water.

Carlisle Journal, 4 May 1844

The Railway

Right: The passenger facilities at London Road were finally demolished in 1881. Only the Railway Hotel on London Road remains as a reminder of the place where railway passengers first alighted in Carlisle. The Railway Hotel had a fine garden which extended to the North Eastern Reading Room, which was reached by a flight of stone stairs .

Below: Goods Depot workers for the North Eastern Railway (date unknown).

Below Right: **1 September 1939**

As war became inevitable, arrangements were made to house evacuees from areas most likely to be bombed and Carlisle offered to take 7,000......The first wave arrived in the City on trains which stopped at the old London Road Station. There were 3,600 of them, some children with adults but most on their own.........they didn't know whether to feel excited or bewildered. Many simply wept...

Carlisle at War, 1929-1945, David Hay.

Leaving Threatened Homes
Refugee children Arrive to-day and to - morrow
Reception Plans for Carlisle and County

CARLISLE is ready to play its part in the evacuation taking place today and tomorrow. Plans are perfected for receiving 3,596 school children and their accompanying attendants during this afternoon and evening. They come from Newcastle and will be followed tomorrow by adults.

The recent accommodation survey of the city revealed voluntary offers to accommodate 7,307 persons, comprising 5,848 unaccompanied children, 260 teachers and helpers, and 1,199 others. Should compulsory powers be granted accommodation can be found for 10,644 persons.

The ward accommodation is as follows:- Stanwix, 1793; Rickergate, 650; Aglionby, 1,275; Greystone, 1,171; St. Nicholas. 936; Currock, 1677; Denton Holme, 687; St. Cuthbert's. 900; Caldewgate, 701; Newtown, 854.

This total of 10,644 does not include accommodation for a further 707 persons which can be found in houses where the occupiers are out at work all day.

Six train loads of children and attendants will arrive at London Road Goods Station to-day as follows:- 2.18 p.m., with 836 children; 4.18 p.m., 700; 5.23 p.m., 450; 5.23 p.m., 210; 6.18 p.m., 650; 6.46 p.m., 750.

The above times apply to the arrival of trains on Saturday with adult evacuees.

Newcastle Chronicle and Journal

Cumbria Heritage Services, Carlisle Library

Left: Up to **1 January 1863**, when the Newcastle & Carlisle Railway transferred its passenger services into the Citadel Station, four omnibuses were regularly used to carry passengers from the London Road station into Carlisle and on to the Canal Basin. One of these omnibuses was run by the Canal Company. Although no photographs are known of these particular omnibuses one can clearly be seen in J W Carmichael's drawing of 1836, an enlarged section of which is shown here.

Old Greystone (1840s)

With the arrival of the railway with its stations, goods yards and workshops, concentrated to the south of the City of Carlisle, there was a need for workers who needed places to live. The fields were developed into houses, in some places the patterns of the streets follow the old field boundaries and former uses are preserved in the names of the streets. Around this time the first terraced housing was developed on Botchergate at Union Street, which was later demolished in the 1930's and became Rydal Street. To the south east lies the Linton Holme area and that of The Mains and Grayston. Here the community developed, centred on the Greystone Cottages, whilst across the River Petteril, stood the village of Botcherby.

The Graystone lands were part of the lands belonging to the Raven family, whose name is retained in Raven Street and Raven Nook.

Greystone

The Carlisle Directory of **1880** gives an interesting insight into the various occupations of the inhabitants of Greystone.

1.	Patterson Barbara, grocer	23.	Thompson, William, fireman
3.	Routledge, John, labourer	24.	Little, James, irondresser
4.	Wittal, Charles, labourer	25.	Hind, Elizabeth
5.	Brown, Elizabeth	26.	Gill, Mary
6.	Birkett, Thomas, labourer	27.	Oliphant, Joseph, platelayer
7.	Dixon, Mary	28.	Alderson, John, fitter
8.	McBride, James, Plasterer	29.	Hindson, Alfred, cowkeeper
9.	Elliot, Joseph, Grocer	30.	Shaw, James, gardener
10.	Little, Joseph, fitter	31.	Stubbs, Mary
11.	Oliphant, Sarah	32.	Howe, John, steamloom weaver
12.	Sowerby, Robert, grocer	33.	Little, William, labourer
13.	Armstrong Walter, labourer	34.	Hind, Richard
14.	Leck, Henry, weaver	35.	Pattinson, Elizabeth, mill hand
15.	Bell, William, signalman	36.	Richardson, E., labourer
16.	Turnbull, James, cowkeeper	37.	Maxwell, David, labourer
17.	McLearn, James, labourer	38.	Pattinson, Wilson, striker
18.	Shane, Samuel, storekeeper	39.	Cook, William, labourer
19.	Elliot, Walter, cowkeeper	40.	Elliott, John, fireman
20.	Bell James, labourer	41.	Fell, Elizabeth
21.	Horsman, Jane	42.	Lindsey, James, labourer
22.	Corbett, Ann	43.	Turner, William, fitter

Graystone Cottages first appear on the Carlisle Census of 1841. "Old Greystone " as it became known stood well back from the Old Road To Warwick Via Graystone (Greystone Rd.) They were small tenements, with long front yards. There was a green in front and railings round.

The properties housed quite large families, and in some cases lodgers were taken in to help make ends meet.

The conditions were cramped and the fact that some families kept livestock didn't help the unsanitary conditions. 'Nuscience to a certain piggery at Old Greystone.'
Council Minutes **1890/91**

During the early years records show most people living here were paupers. Life began to improve with the establishment of a woollen mill at Ravennook, (1850) which along with the Railway was a main source of employment

Carlisle Journal

The old community of Greystone. These houses were pulled down in 1931 as they were considered unsanitary and it was one of a number of sites considered for a bus station. This plan was later dropped and Corporation housing for old folk was built on the site (see later 'Margaret Creighton Gardens').

Raven 114 Nook

We also see from the **1851** Census that the Children of Old Greystone are referred to as being scholars, this was due to the establishment of a school at Old Greystone by a Mr. Walter Davies ....

School

Greystone 115 116

Family names of Old Greystone..........
Stubbs, Gordon, Blaymire, Donnally, Bowman, Dixon, Graham, Bird, Telford , Eckersley, Clark , Birkett and Oliphant. **117**

57 Mr Walter Davies, Headmaster, of Brook Street.
Carlisle Directory **1858**

Recollections of old Greystone (early 1900's)
and the origins of Little and Ballantyne, Market Gardeners

Recollections - On the corner of Sybil Street and Brook Street stood Mr Lawsons Grocery shop / Post Office (Today Cellar 5). Near to Lawsons was Tom Patersons, a small shop at the corner of the entrance to the row of two roomed houses, known as ' Old Greystone,' which stood opposite the row of houses between Fusehill Street and Furze Street. They stood well back from the road, with a green in front bounded by a wooden fence. Tom Hilton was the owner of the properties. He lived in one of the houses and his mother old Mrs Hilton used to collect the rents each week, giving sweets to the children. Another resident was old Mary Ferguson, who would act as midwife for her neighbours.

To the right of the old cottage properties was Mr Joe Emmerson's Blacksmiths shop, the children would watch him shoeing horses and liked to watch the sparks flying off the Anvil as he worked. He combined this with making wheels and other needs for the farming community. Joe lived on Oswald Street.

Behind 'Old Greystone' was a row of better built properties in which lived a Dairyman called Elliot, and a market gardener named Bowes who produced cheap fruit and vegetables. The gardens and orchard had a wooden fence round them They were bounded by Melbourne Road, Delagoa Street and Sybil Street.

Compiled from Letters to the *Cumberland News* , September 1966 .

Lawson's shop, which later became Mr Styth's shop. This 1938 photograph shows Mr Isaac Styth, the proprietor.

"Old Greystone" was put under a demolition order in December 1930, under the 1930's Housing Act of Slum Clearances. The Properties were said to be in a "dilapidated" condition due to ground dampness, insanitary surroundings and lack of conveniences. The site was among those considered as a possible location for Carlisle's new Bus Depot. It was acquired by the Corporation and is now the site of Margaret Creighton Gardens, which was a scheme in the forefront of better provision for the old folks throughout the Country.

Origins - The 1848 Botchergate Tithe Map shows three fields, Nos 77,78 and 79 which were cultivated as a market garden by Messers. Little & Ballantyne. (This same area was previously show as Wetlands on The Carlisle and The Socage Manor Plan of 1610)

The firm of Little & Ballantyne was not founded by either Little or Ballantyne.

The firm was founded in 1790 by two brothers from

The firm moved to the new building on the viaduct in January 1954.

Edinburgh, William and Thomas Hutton. Shortly after, they established a small shop along with a nursery, covering about an acre of land in lower Botchergate, Carlisle (There used to be a memorial tablet to some of the Hutton Family in Christ Church). The firm became well established and was very successful. When the Hutton brothers retired in August 1840 the business was bought by Messers. John Little & Thomas Ballantyne. Later, around the 1860s, they moved the business away from the area and established a shop at 62 English Street. At the same time the nursery was moved to the gardens of Knowfield House, Stanwix (now the site of Knowefield Park Estate). *Greystone Urban Trail*, Carlisle County Library,

When the business was based in Botchergate Mr Ballantyne lived at Rose Cottage, next to St John's church in London Road. For further information on Little and Ballantyne see Denis Perriam's article, Cumberland News, 4 December 1998.

A Cumbrian Diary - **Nursery Garden** ....One very important business on London Road .....Messrs Little and Ballantyne's Nursery was in the London Road area until well into the 1860s. Their nursery extended from the back of Brook Street to what is now Close Street (Close Street was named after the Dean of that name who lived in Carlisle when the street was formed) and back to where the Workhouse (City General Hospital) now stands. The very streets of the district proclaim what had been there before - Garden Street, Flower Street, Orchard Street. *Cumberland News*, 15 November 1957

Raven Nook Mill (Carlisle Woollen Works) 1850

Tuesday 1 July 1740 .... the grounds of the late Richard Ravens called Graystone Lands.......

An extract from the Tithe of John Henry Rigg, Cumbria Records Office.

Carlisle Woollen Works, Raven Nook Mill, 1850.

John and Joseph Hargraves mill was steam powered. Water was supplied by a Mill Race on The River Petteril. Some buildings can still be seen today.

31 May 1850   - HARGRAVE'S NEW WOOLLEN FACTORY

© Cumbria Heritage Services, Carlisle Library

On Monday last (27th. May) the Mayor and Corporation of Carlisle, with a number of other gentlemen attended, in compliance with an invitation, at the laying of the foundation stone of the new Woollen Factory about to be erected by Messrs. Hargraves in the neighbourhood of Botcherby : The corporation assembled at the Town Hall in the forenoon, and proceeded to the ground headed by Jos. Rome Esq., Mayor,and P.H.Howard Esq., MP for the City. On arriving at the place it was found that a considerable crowd had collected, but a sufficient space had been reserved for the gentlemen of the corporation and other friends; who closed in around the intended site of the "Corner Stone" ....the Mayor took the trowel in hand and proceeded in the most scientific way, amid cheers of the assembled multitude; to say they had met that day on a most important occasion - the laying of the foundation stone of a Woollen Manufactory - a thing long desiderated (sic) in Carlisle, and in which it had been left to Messrs. Hargraves. They had his warmest wishes for their prosperity, and connected with their prosperity that of those who might be under their employment, for they could not prosper without being the means of diffusing great good throughout the district. (cheers). They were surrounded by an agricultural, wool-growing district, and he had little doubt that, amongst others, the sheep farmers would reap the benefit of the establishment of such factories. They had long enjoyed the advantages of cotton manufacture, and it was hoped that this was the beginning of a similar course of prosperity for the County of Cumberland in the matter of Woollen Manufacture (cheers). The facilities afforded by Railways and other modern improvements were in their favour. They had water and everything else requisite for the successful prosecution of the work; and last though not least they had a population, which, for Industry and Intelligence was not to be excelled in any part of the Kingdom, who were ever ready to make themselves serviceable if they only receive a fair wage and a fair amount of work...... The outdoor proceedings being concluded, the company were conducted to a marquee which had been erected for the purpose of their accommodation, where they were treated to an excellent glass of wine accompanied by other good and necessary things.

Raven Nook as seen today from a similar viewpoint to the engraving above.

Mr Steele begged to propose a toast to the architect, Mr Hodgson and the contractors .... they were well known in the City.............it was but a re-establishment of this branch of industry here, for it had been introduced about 100 years ago by a number of Flemmings and Germans who came over to this neighbourhood.

Carlisle Journal

28 February 1851 - Carlisle Woollen Factory - It will be in the recollection of our readers that on the 27th May, 1850, the foundation of a new Woollen Factory was laid at Botcherby Mill, near this City, by Joseph Rome Esq., then Mayor. The building, and greater part of the establishment, having been completed, Messr. Hargraves, the enterprising proprietors, invited a party of gentlemen, on Friday morning last to see the machinery set in motion. The High Sheriff, G.H.Head Esq., the Under Sheriff, S.Saul,Esq., Mr Jos. Ferguson, (Fisher Street) Mr. Chance, of Birmingham, Mr Jos.Rome, Mr Bendle, Mr Steele, and a party of ladies, assembled at the works shortly after twelve o.clock, and were received by Mr. J.Hargraves, who conducted them through the building to witness the various operations of sorting, teasing,, carding,, spinning,, weaving, dyeing etc., and explained the successive processes. The engine house, the fulling house, and the gas works, were also inspected, and the visitors appeared

highly interested and delighted with the completeness of all the arrangements. The buildings cover nearly an acre of ground ; and as the works, when in full operation will afford employment to from 200 to 300 hands, the success of the undertaking becomes a matter of great importance to the Town.......The only circumstance that occurred to mar the pleasure of the gathering was, an unfortunate accident to Mr. Boak, who, whilst adjusting a belt for driving part of the machinery, received a severe injury to three fingers of his left hand - the back sinews being completely cut through. We are glad to hear that he is progressing favourably towards recovery, and that the injury he sustained will not prevent him discharging the duties of his situation.

Carlisle Journal

Raven Nook from the north side, in Jesmond Street, as seen today.

Raven Nook Mill (continued)

The Census of **1861** shows that the Woollen Factory manager, George Thwaites was living at 123 Ravennook. Several employees lived at Ravennook and "Old Greystone " Cottages. The census records: 3 Woollen Weavers, 1 Fireman at Woollen Factory, 1 Boot and shoe repairer, 1 Carpenter, 1woollen Factory Manager... George Thwaites.

Railway Wrappers, Coat linings and Horse rugs were just some of the Woollen products manufactured here at this time.

13 March 1872. Hargraves Woollen Mill was offered for sale but was withdrawn due to lack of interest.

.... The Raven Nook Woollen Mill, on Sale - This Mill was advertised for sale in the County Hotel, Carlisle yesterday afternoon, by Mr. Hardy; but it was not offered. It is now open for sale by private treaty.   *Carlisle Patriot.*

28 June 1872. Sale of Raven Nook Woollen Mill - This Woollen Mill situate at Raven Nook, near this City, and carried on for many years by the firm of J and J Hargraves and Co., has been purchased by Mr.Robert Graham, of Brampton and Faugh Beeches. managing director of the Brampton Tweed Mill from its commencement. Mr. Graham has made the purchase on his own behalf, and he intends to remodel the appliances of the establishment for the production of tweed such as is turned out at Langholm, Brampton,and other places............. *Carlisle Patriot.*

24 March 1874. FIRE AT THE CARLISLE SCOTCH TWEED MILL.

Shortly after six o.clock, last Saturday morning the people of Carlisle were roused from their slumbers by the steam-buzzer, whose office as a fire alarm is now pretty well known. On inquiry it was ascertained that Mr. Graham's Tweed Mill at Raven Nook was on fire and thither the fire engines of the Police and of the Volunteer Fire Brigade hastened with very commendable speed. It appears that about twenty minutes to six the watchman, who lives upon the premises, noticed smoke or flames issuing from the wool-sorting room, which contained, beside a large quantity of wool, some reserve machinery in store. He at once went and got the extincteur (sic) which is kept ready charged upon the premises, and directed it with good effect upon the burning mass; and it is his opinion that if he had a second extincteur, he would have suppressed the fire altogether. By this time the work people were arriving, and they set energetically to work with buckets of water. The two fire engines reached the scene shortly afterwards, and though the danger was then pretty well at an end, they put a period to all further suspense by absolutely extinguishing the fire. The wool-sorting room is gutted and unroofed, and all its contents destroyed. In the adjoining finishing-house, the stored yarn and pieces of goods in a raw state suffered considerable damage; and the contents of the room below were much injured by the water. The loss is estimated at a little under £2000. The stock and premises are amply insured. How the fire originated it is impossible to say; probably it arose from a smouldering spark. But for the hearty way in which the workmen turned to with buckets, and for the promptness of the brigades, the entire premises must have been destroyed; and Mr. Graham desires to thank them all for their valuable services which fortunately were successful in confining the area of flames.

Carlisle Patriot.

Council Minutes 1889 / 90

At this time the weaving sheds belonging to the Raven Nook Mill were reported to be dilapidated and in ruinous condition and thought to be dangerous to passers by. Mr. James Graham Esq. was instructed by the council to pull the said buildings down or meet the costs of repair......

21 August 1901

Gentlemen ,

Mr Laing's Property in Raven Street

We have examined the property in Raven Street now belonging to Mr John Laing and excluding ten houses sold to Mr. Solomon Wood and the three sold to Mr J W Laing and find them to comprise:

(Continued at the top of the next page)

Ashley Kendall

Ridley's chemists manufactured mineral waters in part of the mill sometime after the fire of 1874. See above and the ginger beer bottle to the left.

1880	RAVEN NOOK
Graham & Thompson, Scotch Tweed Mills	
Sinclair, James, Clerk	
Heslop, John, Pressman and Caretaker	
1. Ritson, William, Dyer	
2. McDougal, James, Carder	
3. Nixon, James, Weaver.	
4. Saddler, John, Engineman	
5. Ferguson, David, Carder	
6. Paisley, David, Finisher	
7. Thompson, Edward, Joiner	
8. Hodgson, Mrs.	
9. Morans, Mrs.	
10. Bell, Robert, Foreman Weaver	
Botcherby Flour Mills,	
Thomas Bell ,Proprietor....................	
Carlisle Directory 1880.	

Raven Nook Neighbourhood, 1900 on

Mrs Marie Johnston

1. Seven houses of a superior class for Artisan occupation providing :- Sitting room with separate passage, kitchen, scullery, 2 good bedrooms and a very excellent attic, self contained yard with wash house, coal house, and out offices.

2. Five sites now vacant for houses similar to the above.

3. We are of opinion that the houses will let for 6/9 per week when completed and decorated.

4. The property is in a developing situation, is well built and finished and of a class suitable both for letting and selling.

5. We find the value of the whole property to be the sum of £1900, and advise a Trustees Mortgage advance of £1260.   Messrs. Wright Brown & Strong , Solicitors , Carlisle.

20 September 1902 ....The five houses now being erected, when complete, we are of opinion are worth £270 each, *Messrs Wright Brown & Strong, Solicitors, Carlisle .*

courtesy *Rachel Rodway, solicitor, Burnetts , Carlisle)*

Recollections of Raven Nook

Charlie and Anne Davidson

Mrs Marie Johnston (nee Surtees.) aged 75 years, was born in 1922 at No.1 Raven Street, and lived there until she married at the age of 27 years.

Marie attended Norman Street School. Marie's father, Alfred Surtees was a regular of The Linton Holme Hotel. Marie recalls that opposite their house on Raven Street was a field with swings and a sandpit. The houses of Greystone Road backed onto this field and people would hang out their washing here. It was on this land that 28 dwellings for the aged were erected, becoming known as Raven Nook.

Marie recalls Mr. Johnston, the Cowkeeper at Botcherby Mill Farm would chase the children with big sticks, for tormenting his cows. She also recalls the Morton, Alexander carpet factory at Jesmond Street (formerly the woollen factory of 1850). A chap called Charlie Davidson mended mangles, and another man named Carlyle mended Singer Sewing Machines in the buildings next to the Carpet Factory. Marie recalls Dick Irving, father of Bill and Eric, who had a coal yard at the end of Raven Street. The Children nicknamed Mr. Irving " Dick Death," as he was always chasing the children for playing rounders on the spare land. The river ran along the bottom of Raven Street in those days, it used to flood an awful lot. Marie remembers one year the children had to go from the end of Greystone Road to Norman Street School by boat.

During the red hot summers the children spent their days playing around the fields and a beck, before Botcherby Housing Estate was built. She recalls the weir and water fall (the old mill race) next to the carpet factory. "We would sit on the concrete slabs and dangle our feet into the crystal clear waters, sometimes the water would dry up in really hot summers. We didn't like it when they altered the River Petteril. None of us had much money in those days, but they were good times and everyone knew everybody."

June 1978   Irvings Coaches purchased part of the site of Raven Nook Mill from the Appleyard Group Ltd..

Raven Nook in 1937
Marie (Surtees) Johnston is on the right, her sister is centre and her brother is in the front.

Remains of the weir showing the concrete slabs where Marie and her friends would dangle their feet into the "crystal clear" water.

Brook Street & the Turnpike Road

1858 The notice opposite, regarding the re-location of the Harraby Tollgate on London Road, was posted.

The road *"commonly called the Warwick Road"* in the notice is in fact Brook Street and the toll gate was to be located at the junction of London Road and Brook Street.

The Harraby Toll Cottage, further up London Road, is now bricked up but can still be seen. In 1991 it appeared as shown below.

The city authorities demanded that turnpike toll gates should be two miles

Denis Perriam

Carlisle, Penrith, & Eamont Bridge

TURNPIKE ROAD.

NOTICE IS HEREBY GIVEN,

That a Special Meeting of the Trustees of the Turnpike Road under an Act passed in the eleventh year of the reign of King George the Fourth, entitled, an Act for more effectually "repairing the Road from Carlisle to Penrith, and from Penrith to Eamont Bridge, in the County of Cumberland," will be holden at the Crown Hotel, in Penrith, in the said County, on Thursday, the 28th day of October, 1858, at 3 o'clock in the Afternoon, for the purpose of revoking an order of the said Trustees, made at a Meeting held at Penrith, on Tuesday, the 24th day of August last, for removing the Harraby Toll Gate, and erecting another on the said Road. And also, after the revocation of the said Order, for the purpose of determining whether the Toll Gate or Turnpike Gate now erected and being on and across the said Turnpike Road, at Harraby, shall be removed from its present site, and another Turnpike Gate in lieu thereof, be placed at the South corner of a House now occupied by Richard Ormand, Provision Dealer, fronting upon the said Turnpike Road, and situate at or near the South Corner of the Highway commonly called the Warwick Road (being North of Harraby aforesaid), and so from the said South Corner of the House, occupied by the said Richard Ormand, over, upon, and across the said Turnpike Road.

Dated this 5th day of October, 1858.

W. BROUGHAM,
JOHN JAMESON,
J. S. MULCASTER,
WILLIAM IRVING, } Trustees of the said Turnpike Road.

H. BROWN, PRINTER, PENRITH.

from the city centre, London Road formed part of the Carlisle to Kempley Bank (Penrith) turnpike and the toll gate had been moved from the St. Nicholas junction with Botchergate to Harraby in 1830. When the turnpike company proposed a gate closer to the city, at the corner of Brook Street, there was such a public outcry that the plan had to be abandoned.

On this plan of 1844 Brook Street is referred to as Warwick Road. This was an abbreviation of "*The old road to Warwick via Graystone*"

The position of the new tollgates are marked on the map. It is interesting to note that the gates were generally referred to as "*the nuisance*" by the local populace.

1862

Brook Street housing began to be developed. Brook Street took its name from the brook which used to flow along here. The brook was enclosed by a pipe which fed a well. The people of the area would use a hand pump to raise the water from the well.

This wood guide-post sign from the corner of London Road and Brook Street, indicating 4 miles to Warwick Bridge, directed traffic towards the Botcherby Toll Gate along Greystone Road. It dates from 1829/30. Originally the letters would be painted on in white, thus protecting the wood below from the weather. Over the years this has caused an embossed effect as the surrounding wood has been worn away.

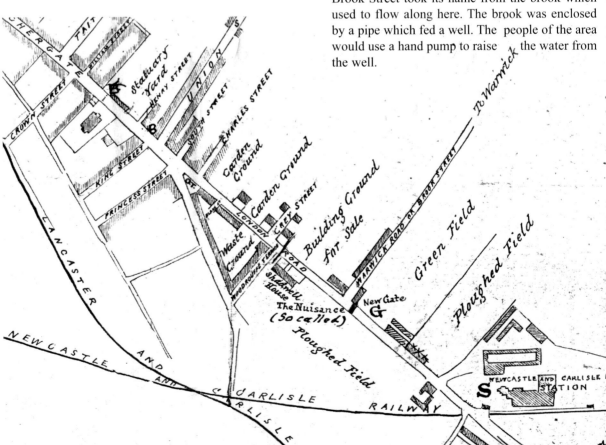

Cowan's Sheldon & Co. Ltd. Est. 1846
St Nicholas Works (1857-1987)

The ploughed field shown near the new tollgates on the map on the previous page was not to remain a ploughed field for long. Within a few years this field was to be home to one of the most prestigious firm of crane makers ever to exist. The two partners who gave the firm its name were John Cowans and Edward Pattinson Sheldon. Both had served their apprenticeships with the firm of Robert Stephenson and Co., makers of *The Rocket* In fact Edward Sheldon, representing Stephenson's Company, had the honour of driving the first locomotive into Carlisle at the opening of the Newcastle-Carlisle railway.

Cowan and Sheldon chose to establish their factory in Carlisle as the coming of the railways was creating new opportunities for trade in the heavy engineering industry. Their first factory was developed in premises at Woodbank, Upperby which had previously been a Calico Print Works. Woodbank lies on the bank of the River Petteril, which provided water power for a Tilt Hammer used by the firm. There was also a small iron foundry at Woodbank worked mainly by a third partner, William Bouch, who had been a fellow apprentice with both Cowan and Sheldon at Robert Stephenson's. William and his more famous

Edward Pattinson Sheldon born at Jarrow-on-Tyne in 1815

John Cowans, born at Bedlington, Northumberland in 1816

Woodbank, Upperby - former Calico Print Works - where Cowan, Sheldon and Bouch established their business in 1846.

younger brother, Sir Thomas Bouch, were both born at the Ship Inn at Thursby. They joined Cowan and Sheldon's Woodbank firm as sleeping partners. Thomas's increasing work as a Civil Engineer created a lot of work, much of which was directed to his brother at Woodbank. Railway wagons, wheels and axles were manufactured as well as machinery and metalwork for the local collieries at Blenkinsop, Kirkhouse, Aspatria and many others. By 1853 this type of work had increased beyond the capacity of Woodbank and the whole of the forge work was transferred to the Darlington Forge. Thomas Bouch went on to become famous as a railway pioneer building the Belah and Deepdale viaducts, the Cockermouth, Penrith and Keswick lines, and the world's first floating railway.

His final achievement was the building of the Tay Bridge, which led to his knighthood and unfortunately to an early death. Only 19 months after completion the bridge collapsed while carrying a train leaving, 75 people dead. Although an enquiry blamed poor workmanship, not the design, for the disaster, Bouch took the brunt of public outrage and retired to Moffat, where he died in 1880, a broken man. A commemorative plaque to Sir Thomas Bouch can be seen on the wall of the Ship Inn at Thursby.

June 1857 Cowan's continued to operate the Woodbank plant until its closure in 1869. In 1857, however, they purchased the site of the St Nicholas Works for £3010 as reported in the Carlisle Journal of **19 June 1857**, see right. The main buildings had been erected only a few years earlier and included foundaries, engineer's fitting shops, sawmills and smithies. The works also had sidings which connected to the Newcastle and Carlisle Railway, thus giving access to the other existing railways. With this development George Dove came into the firm as General Manager and E P Sheldon took on the accounts and office business. On the closure of Woodbank in 1869, a large gunmetal bell, used to call the men to work at Woodbank, was placed on a mount in the reception at the St. Nicholas site. The words "Jesus, Mary, Joseph, 1746" on the bell casting show its previous use.

SALE OF MR. G. D. RICHARDSON'S PREMISES-- The extensive buildings and land at St. Nicholas, in this city, where Mr. G. D. Richardson has carried on the business of waggon builder, &c., for some time, were brought to the hammer on the 11th inst., by order of the assignees under the fiat of bankruptcy, Mr. Browne, of the firm of Messrs. Brown and Son, our townsmen, acting as auctioneer. Several gentlemen from Newcastle and the west of Cumberland were present. The premises, including the heavy fixed machinery, were put up by a gentleman at £1,200, and remained stationary for some little time at £1,400, but on the auctioneer declaring a sale at £2,500, the biddings became more spirited, and, after a severe contest, were finally knocked down to Messrs. Cowan, Sheldon and Co., of Woodbank, at £3010. Several gentlemen expressed their approbation of the manner in which the sale had been conducted. We hear that the remaining portion of the machinery, stock-in-trade, and work tools will shortly be announced for sale on the premises.

Carlisle Journal, 19 June 1857

Cowan's Sheldon & Co. Ltd. Est. 1846
St Nicholas Works (1857-1987)

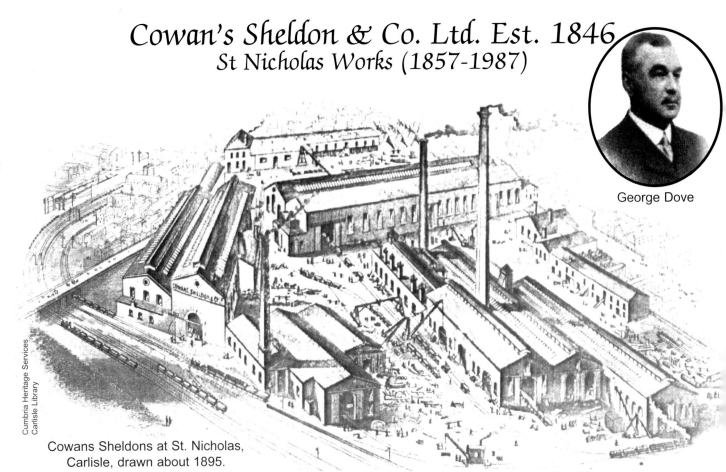

Cowans Sheldons at St. Nicholas,
Carlisle, drawn about 1895.

George Dove

The new, much larger works at St. Nicholas enabled Cowans Sheldon to take on bigger and more prestigious contracts. Cranes were now manufactured, sixty four steam engines were built, and the firm was the first to make turntables on the balance on centre principle.

George Dove's success in his post led to him being made a partner in 1863 from which time he took an important part in the development of the firm, which continued to prosper.

The progress of the firm is amply illustrated by articles which appeared in the local newspapers describing particular engineering successes. The cutting below from the *Carlisle Patriot* of 11th March 1858 describes an enormous set of shear legs, which were constructed by Cowan Sheldon for H. M. Dockyard at Devonport.

A LOCAL ENGINEERING WORK.

Messrs Cowans Sheldon and Co., of the St. Nichola Works, Carlisle, have constructed an enormous set of shear legs, which were erected at H.M. Dockyard, Devonport, last week, and are for use in lifting guns or heavy machinery. They are capable of lifting a heavier weight than any other set in Her Majesty's dockyards. With recent developments the necessity for a structure capable of lifting a mass of material varying from 100 to 150 tons in weight has become a necessity, especially on the sea front, where the largest ships in the Navy could lie. The contract for the huge mass of tubular steel was given to Messrs Cowans, Sheldon and Co. Piece by piece the three legs were welded and rivetted together in the yard, the material having been conveyed there in bulk. The onerous work of lifting the gigantic structure, weighing about 120 tons, was begun on Friday. The operation was an anxious one, as will be imagined when it is stated that in addition to the weight to be raised the two side legs are just 158ft. in length, and the back leg is 202ft. long, and fitted with steps, guarded by rails, for its extreme length. The operation of lifting occupied just 5 hours and 50 minutes, and was watched at intervals by a large staff of officials, among them the Naval Commander in Chief (Admiral the Hon. Sir E. R. Fremantle) and the Admiral Superintendent of the yard (Rear-Admiral H. J. Carr). The work was completed without mishap. Steam winches, and a set of temporary shear legs in the main did the work. Viewed as it now stands, it seems almost incredible that such a mass could have been got into position with such ease. Certain it is that the legs will be the subject of wonderment of passers up and down the river for some time. In the afternoon men were busily engaged fitting the screw, which will enable the legs to travel a distance of 60ft. out of centre, and to lift a weight of 150 tons. An account of the erection is given in the *Western Daily Mercury* of last Saturday.

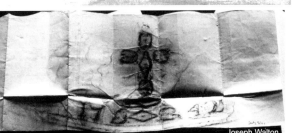

Joseph Walton

Left: from the earliest days Cowans was very keen to develop export markets in the developing countries. This 15 ton hand powered crane for the Nigerian Railways illustrates this well.

The bell tower, top right, contained the bell from Woodbank, prior to its installation in the reception area.

Joseph Walton

Above and below: brass rubbings from the bell.   Above: The Woodbank Bell

JESUS ✠ MARIA ✠ JOSEPH

Cowan's Sheldon & Co. Ltd. Est. 1846
St Nicholas Works (1857-1987)

CRANES of all types, for all purposes

60-ton Floating Crane supplied to the South African Railways and Harbours, Capetown.

We also manufacture other Railway, Dock and Harbour Equipment, including the following:—
WHARF CRANES, CAPSTANS, SLIPWAY HAULAGE WINCHES, LOCOMOTIVE AND WAGON TURNTABLES, LOCOMOTIVE, CARRIAGE AND WAGON TRAVERSERS, WHEELDROPS.

COWANS SHELDON & CO. LTD.

CARLISLE • ENGLAND

LONDON OFFICE
AFRICA HOUSE, KINGSWAY W.C.2.

TEL:-CARLISLE 13 & 14   TEL:-HOLBORN 0268

Although Cowans Sheldon soon became known as *'The Cranemakers'* they also made a large variety of other heavy engineering equipment destined for dock and railway use. The advertisement on the left is from the Carlisle Industrial Exhibition catalogue of 1933

The photograph below of a steam crane was taken at the north east corner of the site about 1936. The chimneypots of Woodruff Terrace can be seen on the left and Shadwell Lodge, which was demolished in 1952 can be seen in the background.

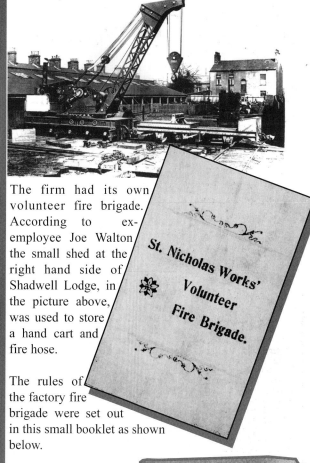

The firm had its own volunteer fire brigade. According to ex-employee Joe Walton, the small shed at the right hand side of Shadwell Lodge, in the picture above, was used to store a hand cart and fire hose.

The rules of the factory fire brigade were set out in this small booklet as shown below.

St. Nicholas Works' Volunteer Fire Brigade.

RULES

1.—The Brigade shall be called "The St. Nicholas Works Volunteer Fire Brigade."

2.—The services of members will be entirely voluntary.

3.—A drill will be held once a month.

4.—No excuse will be accepted for absence from drills, excepting sickness or working overtime.

5.—If an outbreak of fire occurs during working hours the alarm will be given to each Fire Brigade man.

During World War 1 the production of the company was concentrated on work for the Admiralty, War Office Ministry of Munitions and other Government departments. In 1926, the year of the General Strike, the company had to close down for a time due to the lack of coal and as a result experienced financial difficulties. By 1930 business was booming but, by 1933 a recession in the engineering industry caused further problems. The advent of World War 2 saw many of the workers conscripted into the services and the company commenced the production of military equipment, tank parts and heavy lifting gear.

During the 1950s there was a continual struggle to maintain delivery dates and there were cash flow problems. This led, in 1961, to Cowans Sheldon being absorbed by the Glasgow based firm, Clyde, Crane and Booth. Later in 1968 as part of Clarke Chapman it became a subsidiary of the Northern Engineering Industries group. Only eighteen years later, in October 1986, the decision was taken to end manufacturing in Carlisle, although there was enough work to carry on into the 90's. This work was transferred elsewhere and sadly on 6 October 1987 the last giant crane to be manufactured in Carlisle left the premises and is shown overleaf. Now the only reminder is at St Nicholas of this once world famous company is the public house on the east side of London Road, now named "The Cranemakers," but previously known as "The Theakston."

Cowan's Sheldon & Co. Ltd. Est. 1846
St Nicholas Works (1857-1987)

The last crane on its transporter takes up the whole road as it leaves the works at St. Nicholas, Carlisle

On **6 October 1987** Cumberland Evening News industry reporter, Gareth Moore, described the departure of the last crane to be built at the St. Nicholas factory on its journey to India. The rail crane, weighing 158 tons, was expected to take between two and four days to travel to Barrow Docks, where it was to be embarked on a ship for India. It was a sad moment for the spectators, many of whom had finished the previous Friday after years of service with Cowans. This marked the end of a tradition of crane-making which stretched back to 1825. Only a handful of staff remained to tidy up the London Road site before they too were to lose their jobs. Twenty eight design and sales staff were to be kept on and a further eleven cranes, made from parts manufactured in Carlisle, were to be built in India. The parts were to be shipped out before the end of the month.

Joe Walton

Happier times at Cowan's Sheldon. This 1976 staff photograph was taken to celebrate the completion of an order for the Iraqi State Railways.

The nameplate of a 10 ton crane built in 1905 at Carlisle by Cowan's Sheldon & Co. Ltd..

Cumbria Heritage Services, Carlisle Library

Fusehill, the Union Workhouse (1863)

There had been a workhouse in Botchergate prior to the building of St Cuthbert's workhouse at Harraby Hill in 1809. Then, in 1834, the Poor Law Unions took relief responsibilities away from Parishes and all of the workhouses in the area were administered by a Board of Guardians. In 1862 the Board of Guardians decided to build a new workhouse to accommodate everyone, rather than have three workhouses.

The Fusehill Union Workhouse was erected in 1863 and opened in April 1864. The workhouse covered an area of about 7 acres and was built in an Italianate style. The workhouse could accommodate about 500 poor men, women and children.

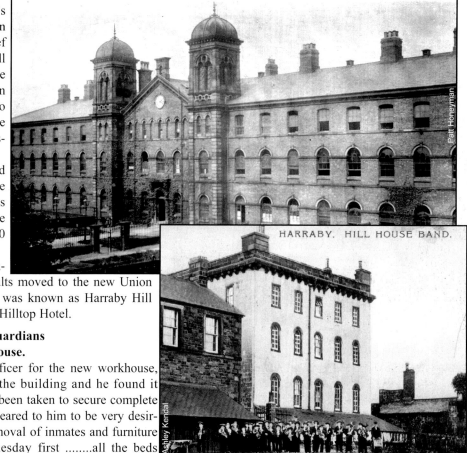

St. Cuthbert's Workhouse, however, continued in use for poor children when the adults moved to the new Union Workhouse. St. Cuthbert's, pictured right, was known as Harraby Hill House and stood on the site of the modern Hilltop Hotel.

Carlisle Board of Guardians
The New Workhouse.

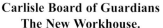

Dr. Hall, the newly appointed medical officer for the new workhouse, reported that he had carefully inspected the building and he found it quite fit for occupation. Great pains had been taken to secure complete ventilation.....the general arrangements appeared to him to be very desirable.....it was determined to commence removal of inmates and furniture from Coal Fell Hill (Caldewgate) on Tuesday first ....all the beds should be put up in the new house ready for occupying the same night....... remarks were made about the supply of milk and the extra expense incurred in it's delivery at the new Workhouse, involving the dismissal of a donkey and the purchase of a pony on the part of the contractor. *Carlisle Journal.*, **4 March 1864**

THE NEW POOR-HOUSE

Crabbe in his description of the parish poor house of his time, speaks of it as the abode of misery-walls of mud, broken doors, putrid vapours, the hum of the dull wheel through the day, the abode of parents who know no children's love, heart broken matrons, foresaken wives, mothers never wed, dejected widows, crippled, aged, the lame, the blind, the moping idiot, the groans of suffering, the last sigh, and, finally the hasty consignment to the earth of him or her " whom nobody owns ".

To this the new Carlisle Union Poor-House, lately opened presents a perfect contrast......A refuge for the Destitute, home for the needy, aged and helpless childhood; in a word the "Palace of the Poor".....an inspection of the interior .....ample space, careful ventilation, cleanliness, health, comfort and evident

content.... The adult poor, and very young children in the care of their mothers, lately in the workhouses at the Castle Bank, Coalfell Hill and Harraby Hill have been removed into their new quarters, with the exception of children of age to be separated from their parent.......about a hundred, are continued at Harraby Hill.

On Tuesday evening - a time of general holiday - the event of entering into possession was celebrated by an appropriate festival in a small way. Kind friends, by subscription amongst themselves, supplied the creature comforts in the shape of tea and cakes. At five o'clock the juvenile inmates of Harraby Hill establishment marched down to the new house headed by the boys' drum and fife band; and at half past five, two hundred and seventy five of all ages men, women and children, were seated at the tables

in the new dining room. They were waited upon by several members of the Board of Guardians ....the room is fitted up to serve the double purpose of Salle-a-manger and chapel. The tables are arranged in two rows, and afford accommodation for more than five hundred person ..It had been announced that the Dean would preach in honour of the occasion, and a considerable number of visitors were admitted by ticket. The Very Reverend Gentleman, however, was prevented by a severe cold and partial loss of voice.....the Rev. Mr. Karney, in his surplice, read the evening church service. The musical part of it had the aid of a well played harmonium ....The proceedings terminated about eight o' clock, when the visitors retired....

Carlisle Patriot, **2 April 1864**

CARLISLE BOARD OF GUARDIANS
COMPLETION AND COST OF NEW WORKHOUSE

The Clerk read a letter from the architects of the New Workhouse, reporting the completion of the works.......They reported that the works had been executed in a fair, sound, and workmanlike manner. The building had been erected about three months sooner than the time specified. The accounts of the contractors were then read,and the extras that had been incurred........ The total cost of the building has been £13,027. this is exclusive of the cost of the land, the furniture, the architects commission and Clerk of the works' salary, and would amount in whole to about £14,727. *Carlisle Journal,* **15 April 1864**

Patt Honeyman

Left: An early view of the infirmary area of the original Fusehill workhouse. This building now houses the City Maternity Hospital.

CARLISLE BOARD OF GUARDIANS.
The fortnightly meeting of the Guardians of this union was held in the board room of the new workhouse, yesterday (Thursday) ....A committee appointed to consider the dietary at the new workhouse, reported that they recommended boiled rice with treacle sauce and white bread should be substituted for the suet pudding for Saturday's dinner........it was found that four ounces of boiled rice filled a quart basin but some of the inmates did not seem to relish the change.......the suet pudding was far too heavy for the old and infirm inmates and the boiled rice, it was considered was a very nice light wholesome food..........the rice and sauce were very nice but the addition of milk would make it more palatable and certainly more nutritious......It was agreed to allow all the old inmates who could be trusted, to attend church or chapels of their own religious denominations on Sunday mornings. ....The board adjourned at 5 o' clock.

Carlisle Journal. **13 May 1864.**

Cumbria Heritage Services, Carlisle Library

Left: The Board of Guardians of the Fusehill Workhouse. The lady in the centre with the white apron was Nurse Parker, the first district nurse.

Below: Detail from the plan showing the allocation of rooms on the south wing of the second upper floor of Fusehill Workhouse. Note the writing on the plan indicating the 'Disorderly Womens' Bedrooms' !

26 December 1899

"Christmas Day was spent in the usual way at both the Carlisle workhouses. The guardians provided a dinner of roast beef and plum pudding at both Fusehill and Harraby Hill, and in addition there were many seasonable gifts to both houses from friends outside.

In the house and hospital at Fusehill there are 238 inmates (of whom 91 are in the hospital), as compared with 256 last Christmas and 273 the year before. For this numerous family the master and matron, Mr and Mrs Scott, cooked 29 stones of beef, 30 stones of potatoes, and 42 stones of plum pudding; and in addition to this excellent dinner breakfast consisted of tea and plain and currant buns, and

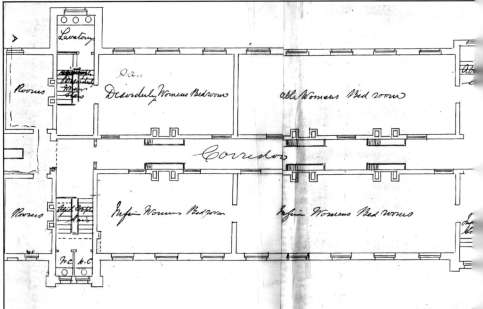

there were currant cakes for tea......the dining hall was bright with evergreens, artificial flowers, mottoes etc......those who sent gifts to the inmates.... Sir Wilfred Lawson, evergreens........Mr. Cookson, 6lbs tobacco, Mrs. Crosthwaite, tea and sugar for the old women, Mrs. Stephenson, toys for the children: Messrs. W Oram and Sons, oranges and apples for the children.........the P.S.A. Society, toys for children, Mr R. Stewart, cards and pennies for children. All the smokers also received and ounce of tobacco each from the Board of Guardians and the non-smokers, tea and sugar. It will thus be seen that everything possible was done to make the day as happy as possible and with the usual discipline relaxed and so many good things available, the day was passed pleasantly by all........ *Carlisle Patriot*

Fusehill, the Union Workhouse (in wartime)

During both world wars the Fusehill Institution was used as a military hospital, as was Brook Street School.
In World War 1 Fusehill was used as an emergency hospital from 16 October 1917 to 5 June 1919

1914-1918   "The Fusehill workhouse was cleared of it's patients and converted into a military hospital, also many large houses and mansions in the City were given to convalescent homes and hospitals ... We knew if there had been extra fighting on the Western Front, as word would go round that ambulances had been running all night to Fusehill and that a lot of patients had been sent to convalescent homes to make room for new cases."

Mildred Edwards 1977

The signing of the Armistice signalling the end of hostilities was a cause for great rejoicing.

Above: Fusehill Hospital was one of the hospitals to receive injured troops from the Gretna rail disaster of 1915. Those well enough to leave their beds posed for a photograph with the nurses on the entrance steps of, what is now the City Maternity Hospital.

REJOICINGS AT PEACE

STIRRING SCENES IN CARLISLE

WORK AT A STANDSTILL

DEMONSTRATIONS IN THE STREETS

The Military hospitals
Nowhere was the news received with greater delight than in the military hospitals. At Fusehill the men on hearing the buzzers raised a hearty cheer and handshaking and congratulations were exchanged. Many of the wounded soldiers were already in the Streets. But many others immediately left the hospital and their example was followed by a large part of the staff.......A number of wounded men at Fusehill paraded the town in the staff motorcar.......,
Carlisle Journal, **12 November 1918**

1939 -1945 World War II
The Fusehill Hospital was one of the first buildings to be sandbagged..... There was a strong protest against the removal of railings from around Fusehill Hospital. People were getting into the hospital grounds and using the air raid shelters "For unpleasant purposes" ....The Maternity wing at Fusehill was a Military hospital in those days, it's four wards taking up to 120 patients, as soon as a bed was emptied it was immediately filled......
"The maternity unit housed the German and Italian wounded soldiers and the main building the British and Canadian soldiers .... they wore a uniform of red ties, white shirts and blue suits, this made them easily recognisable in town and they would be allowed into the Pictures Houses for free..."

George Johnston, Recollections of World War II.

British Red Cross Museum and Archives

Above: Wounded Dunkirk survivors find a haven at Fusehill hospital.

Right:
George Johnston, barber to the soldiers, has also carried on a hairdressing business at 2 Sybil Street for 55 years and his father for 21 years previous to George .

14 August, 1923.

The annual outing of Fusehill inmates to Glenridding, which was arranged by the Guardians Social Committee. *Carlisle Journal.*

Between 1930 and 1950 the area immediately behind the infirmary range was an open-air area known as the "Pavilion." The Pavilion had a canopy above to protect the patients from the elements. Here you would find the Consumption patients who needed fresh air to aid recovery. The worst sufferers were sent into the Lake District to Blencathra Sanatorium.

31 October 1930

Treatment of Tuberculosis

The Health Committee resolved that the Public Assistance Committee be recommended to grant to the Health Committee, the immediate use of the tuberculosis pavilions at Fusehill..... Persona suffering from tuberculosis, would go to those pavilions, where they would be near their friends in the City. *Carlisle Journal.*

Carlisle Journal 14 August 1923

29 December 1931

Left: Christmas day at Fusehill institution - The Master (Mr.Elsdon) is offered the first cut from the beef. *Carlisle Journal*

Pocket Money for Fusehills Aged Inmates
City P.A.C.'s Unanimous Decision

The Carlisle Public Assistance Committee......decided to make a personal allowance of 1s. a week to persons aged over 65 years and over who are inmates of the Fusehill Institution. The cost it was stated, would be about £100 a year... *Carlisle Journal.* **19 July 1938**

With this, being the humble beginnings of Old Age Pensions, the Workhouses were to become a thing of the past. The interior layout of the Fusehill Workhouse dormitories made the building ideal for use as a hospital.

So on **1 June 1937** the workhouse was finally closed and the Fusehill building became the City General Hospital, although some facilities were retained after this date for vagrants and itinerant paupers. The City Maternity Hospital had been at George Street since 1920 and in 1941 an additional maternity unit was opened up on the City General site. This was, and still is, situated in what had been the hospital unit for the Union Workhouse. At the time of writing changes are in the air again and very soon all hospital facilities in Carlisle will be transferred to the Cumberland Infirmary site on Newtown Road, where a new, enlarged hospital is currently being built. Part of the Fusehill building has already been taken over by St. Martin's College, Lancaster and it looks as if the future of the Fusehill building will lie in the development of further education facilities in the city.

31 August 1959

5 May 1963 Below: Marie Kathleen Dickens, was born at Fusehill Maternity Hospital. The first born was always delivered at Fusehill, any further children were delivered at The George Street Maternity Hospital, now demolished.

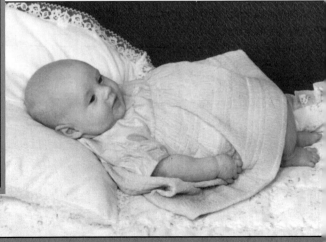

Above: Admiring the television set at the City General Hospital, which was presented on behalf of the Cumberland Friends of Sanatoria Patients by secretary Mr. T. E. Butterworth (fourth left) and received by the Mayor of Carlisle (Mr. W. J. Hunter), who handed it over to the Matron, Miss D. J. Toft (sixth left). *Cumberland Evening News*

Botchergate Recreation Ground (opposite Fusehill)

27 May 1892

BOTCHERGATE RECREATION GROUND.

Botchergate Recreation Ground.

The Botchergate Recreation Ground, is situated at the junction of Fusehill Street, Grey Street, and Back Howe Street, and is little over an acre in size. The site was formerly a gravel pit, which was filled up by the dry rubbish of the City. It could not be utilised for building purposes, and perhaps therefore, it could not have been devoted to a better use than that which it has been dedicated by the corporation. The main idea in laying out the ground was to provide as much open space as possible for the Children to play in. A walk has been formed round the site, and the ground has been enclosed with an ornamental wrought iron unclimbable fence fixed upon a stone base. The whole of the ground has been thoroughly under-drained, and the surface has been covered with a thick coating of gravel upon which has been placed fine crushed Threlkeld granite ....The Gymnasium will be at the West end of the ground, parallel and adjacent to Back Howe Street. The gymnastic apparatus contracted for includes giants stride or round swing, horizontal and parallel bars, ordinary swings, climbing ladder, vaulting horse, see-saw etc.

The Botchergate Recreation Ground is somewhat of an experiment, and should it be successful, no doubt a demand will arise in other parts of the City for the provision of similar opportunities of play and exercise of the children........Prior to the time fixed for the formal opening the scene presented over all parts of the spacious romping ground was one of wildest excitement. Many hundreds of children of all ages seemed bent upon performing a little opening ceremony on their own account, and all sorts of juvenile games were indulged in..........The band of The Artillery Volunteers played at intervals on a specially erected bandstand in the centre of the playground, and the music was greatly appreciated by the large numbers of adult folk who had gathered together to see the opening ceremony. ..... The chief constable drove up in a Hansom, and almost immediately the Sword and Mace bearers and the Halberdiers took up their position. The Corporation quickly followed and awaited the arrival at the gate of the carriage containing the Mayor, the Bishop and Lord Morpeth..............Mr. Wheatley addressed the Mayor ,and, in handing him a silver key with which to formerly open the gate.......invited him in the name of The Recreation Grounds Sub-Committee of the Health Committee to open the gate...........The key is made of Silver extracted from ore obtained from one of the Cumberland Lead Mines, and was specially designed by Mr Wheatley. It was manufactured on his premises in English Street. The outline of the handle is Gothic and comprises of two C's joined together........the initial letters of the Corporation of the City of Carlisle. It is appropriately decorated with Roses richly embossed (the Rose being the floral emblem of the City and forming part of the heraldic bearings). The same design is continued in the pillar, and the wards are closely covered with fine scroll engraving...........

The Mayor then opened the gate and amid loud cheers proceeded to the platform followed by the rest of the Municipal body and their guests. The rain at this moment came down in torrents but the enthusiasm of the assembled multitude showed no sign of abatement..........

The Mayor said he had much pleasure indeed on an interesting occasion like this in being able to pronounce The Botchergate Recreation Ground open to the public at large. A day like this when they had laid the foundation stone of an institution like Tullie House..............the recreation ground was dedicated to the advantage of the rising generation........

The Bishop of Carlisle, who was cordially greeted said.........in olden times the people used to have the Village Green and they used to surround the Maypole, but now they lived in Towns, and when the children were so hard worked in school, what with the Education Code, and the standards and this and that, it seemed to him that the children wanted more play, and he rejoiced that in Botchergate they had opened such a recreation ground........ringing cheers having again been given for the Mayor and the Bishop, the Corporation left the recreation ground..........the Artillery Volunteer Band continuing to play in the ground for some time.

Carlisle Journal

Left: Grey Street (Fusehill) Bowling Green and Tennis Courts - Today the area is known as Fusehill Gardens.

St John's Church, London Road (1867)

At the turn of the nineteenth century Carlisle had two Parishes only; St. Marys and St. Cuthberts. In 1828, however, a move was made to build a chapel of ease for St. Cuthberts without; the Botchergate-St Nicholas area and in September 1830 Christ Church was consecrated in Botchergate (now open space in between the old cinemas, Studios 1,2,3,4, and Mayblin's, Newsagents). Its parochial limits were later extended to take in much of the area covered in this book. The year 1860 saw a new Bishop consecrated to the Diocese, one Samuel Waldegrave, a man of strong protestant and Evangelical convictions. He urged forward the building of more churches. He was supported by Francis Close, (Close Street's namesake), who was Dean of the Cathedral and a man with similar ideas to the Bishop.

An early photograph of St John's Church

The population had increased up to 9,000, so the "carve up" of St. Cuthberts Without into smaller units began and 1865 saw the consecration of St. Stephens in James Street.

.... The St. Nicholas area comprising it is alleged some 4,500 persons, *principally weavers, mechanics, railway labourers and small shopkeepers* with *but very few gentlemen's houses? These were for the most part strangers to the church.* It was, therefore, *a matter of urgency to provide the Bread of Life and the Water of Salvation for the Spiritual wants of these who so deeply need them.* So it was proposed to *build a free church in this most populous part of the Parish* (St Johns).

Centenary Brochure, St. John the Evangelist, Carlisle
1867- 1967.

12 March 1863.

A preliminary meeting of the St. Nicholas Building Committee was held at the Deanery at 12 noon, and the church, subsequently to be called St. John the Evangelist, was born.

St. John's Anglican Church was erected in 1867 in Victorian Gothic style, situated on the corner of Close Street and London Road. We see from parish records that many of the people living around the Linton Holme and Greystone area worshipped in St. Johns.

St. John's—the Architect's impression

16 June 1979.

A Carlisle church will be knocked down to make way for the City's inner ring road.

St. John the Evangelist Church in London Road along with the Parish hall and Vicarage will be demolished, although no date has yet been set for the construction of the road.

The Rev. Christopher Morris, press officer for Carlisle diocese said " We have not decided yet when the church will be pulled down or where it will be rebuilt.

A spokesman for Carlisle City Council added that plans for the ring road had not been finalised .

Cumberland News.

Needless to say St. John's Church is still there today. Happily, the proposed inner ring road never happened.

The beautiful interior of St John the Evangelist Church in London Road

Origins of Street Names around the Linton Holme

27 November 1880.

On this day before John Giles Mounsey Esq. (Steward of the manor of The Duke of Devonshire Socage) came Charles John Ferguson, devisee named in and by the will of Joseph Ferguson deceased who survived George Ferguson deceased and prayed be admitted tenant of all those 2 acres and a half of arable meadow or pasture ground more or less situate lying and being at a place called Seven Acres ....of the customary rent of 5 shillings.

Court Book 1864 - 1900 . p.64. - Carlisle Records Office.

Preparations are being made to build a number of cottages. Mr. C.J.Ferguson has had three new Streets planned on the field off Brook Street, London Road. Plans are now before the Health Committee. He proposes to name them Lindisfarne Street, Oswald Street, and St. Cuthberts Street.........

*Carlisle Patriot, **22 July 1881**.*

The three Streets proposed by Mr.C.J.Ferguson take their names from the island of Lindisfarne where Mr. C.J.Ferguson, who was an architect, had worked on Bamburgh Castle there.

The name of Linton Street is taken from the much earlier, Lintern Lane. Greystone Road dates from the 1890's and takes it's name from when it was known as The Road To Warwick Via Greystone. Greystone being derived from the names of the fields, The Mains and Graiston Flat.

Marjorie Street and Jackson Street take their names from " The Carlisle Miser " Marjorie Jackson, of Botcherby Mill.
Raven St. / Raven Nook derive their names from the once owners of the land the Raven family. Nook Street is situated close to the Raven Nook Mill.
Adelaide Street, The first building to be erected on Adelaide

Street was around 1899, 11 houses, and a shop and house were built for Messrs Gordon & Logan. Adelaide Street and Melbourne Road probably derive their names from the patriotic zeal for the Empire, engendered during the Boer War. Known locally as Little Australia. 1898 plans exist showing there was the intention to further develop the area which is now Melbourne Park, with street names such as Sydney Road, Montreal Street etc.. Sebergham Terrace, now incorporated in Sybil Street (The houses with front gardens) was built by Laings, who originated from Sebergham. In 1898 to ease the problems of flooding , Greystone Road, between Raven Nook and Brunton Place was widened and raised. Messrs. P & J.W. Hayton acting as trustees for the late Mr. James Graham, dedicated 409 sq. yards or thereabouts of land on condition the corporation would flag the area for free.

Thompson Street and Watson street. These streets take their names from the owners of the land, Thompson Bros. & Watson.
Orchard Street, Flower Street and Garden Street take their names from the old

use of the land as fields of the Nurserymen, Little & Ballantyne.
Warwick Road, part of the new turnpike to Brampton (to replace Greystone Road as the main road to Newcastle), dates from 1829. At first it was called Botcherby Road. The toll gate was situated at the junction of Warwick Road and Greystone Road. The later date of Warwick Road is the reason there are not many hostelries along it.
Delagoa Street was built in the same year as an incident during the Boer War when the British sent a gunboat to the port of Delagoa in Mozambique.

A long straight view and the reason why!
Readers acquainted with the layout of the streets in this area will have noticed how Rydal Street (previously Union Street) forms a very obvious straight line with the tree-lined Broad Street and St. Aidans Road, so that when standing at the eastern end of St. Aidans Road (Stoneyholme), one can see straight through all the way to Botchergate.
The reason for this lies with Carlisle's first water supply. The steam pumping station at Stoneyholme (now demolished) pumped water along an underground pipe, which ran below these streets, to Botchergate. It then followed Botchergate and London Road to the storage reservoir on Harraby Hill. Part of the Harraby Hill reservoir can just be seen at the bottom of the map on page 11 of this book.

Percy Dalton

Mr Percy Dalton had a great influence on the 20th Century development of this area.
The building of Botcherby Council house estate, (1928-1930), Margaret Creighton Gardens, (1931/32), Vasey Crescent (1937) and the alterations to the River Petteril, to alleviate the problem of flooding in 1931, were, just some of the works undertaken under the supervision of Percy Dalton.
Percy Dalton was also the Grandfather of Angus Dalton, a well known regular at the Linton Holme Hotel, see page 96.

21January 1884.
Percy Dalton was born the son of a book-keeper in Walton, in the County of Lancaster, to Margaret and Samuel Dalton.
He joined the Carlisle Corporation in 1909, as architectural assistant to Mr. H.C.Marks, the then City Engineer and Surveyor. His first job was to complete the erection of the Turkish Baths on James Street, his next was the extension of the Electricity Works on the opposite side of James Street (the Enterprise Centre Today), in 1910 and 1913, respectively.
In 1919 Percy Dalton became deputy to Mr Marks, and in September 1926, on Mr Marks retirement Percy Dalton succeeded him

Mr. Percy Dalton A.R.I.B.A. A.M.Inst.C.E. 1884 -1957 City Engineer & Surveyor for Carlisle, seen here at the age of 42 in 1926.

Percy Dalton became a pioneer in housing development, because the building programme upon which the City embarked in 1919, immediately upon the close of the 1914 -18 war, placed Carlisle in the fore front of the municipalities dealing with the housing shortage.
Council Housing estates were opened up in various suburbs. He supervised the Housing programme until his retirement; Twenty two new housing estates were built (including Raffles and Longsowerby). Special designs for old peoples dwellings were also included, such as Margaret Creighton Gardens for the old folk, which was acclaimed from as far afield as Ireland.
He designed and supervised the construction of the railway sidings and buildings of the Electricity Power Station at Willowholme, opened in 1927.
Percy Dalton also designed the extensions for five bridges; The Caldew Bridge, The Eden Bridge, Warwick Road, London Road and St. Nicholas Bridges.
The Police and Fire Brigade H.Q. in Rickergate were also completed under his supervision in 1941.

Carlisle was one of the first authorities to support the establishment of Community Centres and Percy Dalton made a study of their design, his work being recognised by the Social Services.
Percy Dalton was also responsible for the demolition of the Gaol (now Woolworths) and the island block which stood in front of it.

Pleasureland has proved a strong attraction and the boats have been in great demand.

He designed Pleasureland (Hammonds Pond), Heysham Park (Raffles) and the Italian Gardens at the Stanwix end of Eden Bridges. He also played an important part in the Carlisle Pageant in 1928.
In carrying out an extensive City Sewage Scheme he saved the City £17,000. He also oversaw the tarmacadaming of many of the City streets and roads.
It is interesting to note that Hammond's Pond, originally opened in 1922 has, in the winter

Mr Percy Dalton's Appointment

The Council in selecting Mr. Percy Dalton to succeed Mr Marks have acted on the principal of promoting a member of their own staff who has already proved his professional competence by his work in office.......his appointment was criticised by some of the labour members on the ground that so important a post should have been thrown open to public competition..... Mr Percy Dalton's credentials are so strong that no useful purpose would have been served by advertising for other applicants for the post......The fact that only four members of the Council joined in the protest against the appointment tells it's own tale. The objection had no better justification than the argument that Mr Dalton should be paid less than an outsider would have received.......Economy is a virtue, but it is never wise to pay an official filling a responsible post less than the true market value of his services...

Carlisle Journal **17 September 1926**

The advertisement in the Carlisle Journal, 26 June 1925, for the recently opened recreation park at Hammonds Pond

of 1998, undergone a complete renovation, designed to bring it back to its former glory. At the time of writing the work is still in progress. Percy Dalton retired after 40 years service to the city on Thursday 20 January 1949. During his working life he had contributed, perhaps more than any other single person, to the making of Carlisle into the city we know today.

Brook Street School (1891-1999)

1891 Lithograph of the New Boys Girls and Infants Schools, Brook Street
built for the City of Carlisle School Board

Brook Street School for Boys, Girls and Infants was designed by T.Taylor Scott. The school was opened in 1891 with 93 pupils in attendance. As was usual in those days boys and girls were taught separately, not just in separate classrooms but also in separate buildings. The photographs below from a pamphlet produced during Carlisle Education week in 1924 illustrate this well.

NEEDLEWORK CLASS - BROOK STREET GIRLS SCHOOL

A CLASS OF BOYS AT WORK - BROOK STREET

29 May 1928   Empire Day -

The whole of the City of Carlisle celebrated, with many events taking place in the area.

Brook Street Infant School put on their own pageant and the event was recorded in the *Carlisle Journal.*

Brook Street School (1891-1999)

A famous former pupil was the Olympic standard swimmer Doreen Hutton. Doreen's abilities as a swimmer first came to note in newspaper reports of Border City Swimming Club successes in **1936** (See right).

3 August 1939

"When the Royal Scot pulled out of the Citadel Station, Carlisle, today, it carried a sixteen year old Carlisle girl upon whom the hopes of every Carlisle swimmer will hang on Saturday. She is Miss Doreen Hutton, now on her way to swim for England against Germany at Erfurt in the international swimming competitions which are taking place this weekend.... Her successes to date include the British National 440 yds championship, the Argenta Trophy, regarded as the unofficial championship of the North, which she took from Lancashire for the first time, and the 220 yards championship of Cumberland and Westmorland in the record time of 2 minutes 43 seconds, while she has the distinction of being twice Border City champion while still under 14, twice winner of the Cumberland under 14, and the under 14 junior championship." *Carlisle Journal*

Doreen Johnston (nee Hutton) still lives in Carlisle and tells how she taught herself to swim in the River Eden, near to *Johnny Bulldog's Lonning* (adjacent to the Tesco Superstore), where there was a log that she could dive off. Many people would go there to swim and fish (It cost 2d to get into Carlisle Baths then). On her successful return from Germany, where she won for England, she was driven around the avenues of Botcherby to the cheers of everyone. In August 1939 Doreen was looking forward to representing Britain at the 1940 Olympic games at Helsingfors, having been provisionally accepted as one of the British team. However this did not happen as the games were cancelled due to the outbreak of war. Doreen suffered further bad luck immediately after the war, when she was due to swim for England in South Africa. Again this did not happen because of the political situation which prevented her from obtaining a visa. Doreen still swims at Carlisle Baths and helps her friends learn to swim.

Doreen aged 16 after her success at Erfurt

1939.....Immediately war was declared, Carlisle Council announced that £27,250 would be spent on shelters and trenches for 19,000 children and teachers.......An inspection of City school shelters in 1940 revealed that only Brook Street had an acceptable shelter, six feet below ground. All the others were *"mere apologies"* for shelters. .... *Carlisle Prepares for War, Carlisle at War 1939-1945,* David Hay.

1991 saw the centenary of Brook Street School and the occasion was commemorated with the presentation of a photograph showing past pupils of the school who had gone on to become senior Cumbria County Councillors, see below. Carlisle MP Eric Martlew is another noted ex-pupil and two well known footballers were also educated at Brook Street, namely Liverpool football player, Peter Thompson and the famous, Kevin Beattie.

Doreen Johnston (nee Hutton), March 1999.

In recent years Brook Street School housed the Schools Music Service and was the infant school for the area. The nearby Greystone School took the Junior pupils. On the closure of Greystone Junior School in the summer of **1982**, Brook Street School underwent extensions and internal alterations at a cost of £115,000 to convert the school into a 280 pupil, infants and juniors school.

Left: Well known ex pupils of Brook Street School include Cumbria County Councillors, Jim Oswald, Geoff Whalley, Hugh Little OBE, Mary Styth and Nonie Wrightson. This photograph was taken in 1991 to mark the centenary year of the school

Sale of Land for Building, (1891)

Around 1890 there was increased pressure to develop housing in the area and various plots of land were put up for sale.

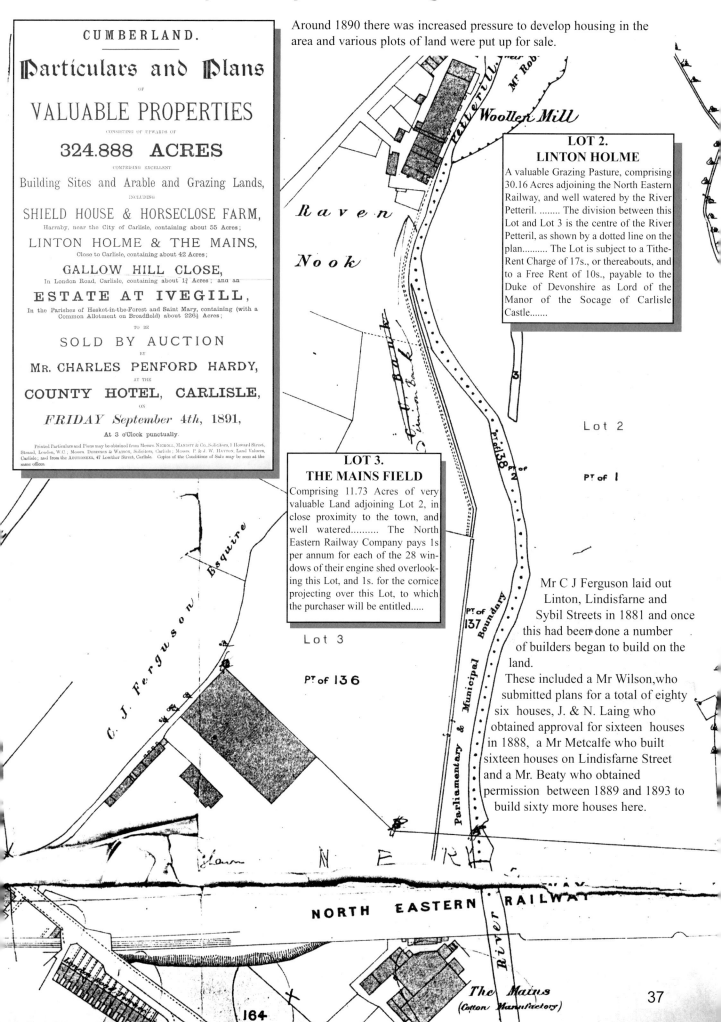

CUMBERLAND.

Particulars and Plans
OF
VALUABLE PROPERTIES
CONSISTING OF UPWARDS OF

324.888 ACRES
COMPRISING EXCELLENT

Building Sites and Arable and Grazing Lands,
INCLUDING

SHIELD HOUSE & HORSECLOSE FARM,
Harraby, near the City of Carlisle, containing about 55 Acres;

LINTON HOLME & THE MAINS,
Close to Carlisle, containing about 42 Acres;

GALLOW HILL CLOSE,
In London Road, Carlisle, containing about 1¾ Acres; and an

ESTATE AT IVEGILL,
In the Parishes of Hesket-in-the-Forest and Saint Mary, containing (with a Common Allotment on Broadfield) about 226½ Acres;

TO BE

SOLD BY AUCTION
BY

Mr. CHARLES PENFORD HARDY,
AT THE

COUNTY HOTEL, CARLISLE,
ON

FRIDAY September 4th, 1891,
At 3 o'Clock punctually.

Printed Particulars and Plans may be obtained from Messrs. NICHOLL, MANISTY & Co., Solicitors, 1 Howard Street, Strand, London, W.C.; Messrs. DOBINSON & WATSON, Solicitors, Carlisle; Messrs. P. & J. W. HAYTON, Land Valuers, Carlisle; and from the AUCTIONEER, 47 Lowther Street, Carlisle. Copies of the Conditions of Sale may be seen at the same offices.

LOT 2.
LINTON HOLME

A valuable Grazing Pasture, comprising 30.16 Acres adjoining the North Eastern Railway, and well watered by the River Petteril. .... The division between this Lot and Lot 3 is the centre of the River Petteril, as shown by a dotted line on the plan.......... The Lot is subject to a Tithe-Rent Charge of 17s., or thereabouts, and to a Free Rent of 10s., payable to the Duke of Devonshire as Lord of the Manor of the Socage of Carlisle Castle.......

LOT 3.
THE MAINS FIELD

Comprising 11.73 Acres of very valuable Land adjoining Lot 2, in close proximity to the town, and well watered.......... The North Eastern Railway Company pays 1s per annum for each of the 28 windows of their engine shed overlooking this Lot, and 1s. for the cornice projecting over this Lot, to which the purchaser will be entitled.....

Mr C J Ferguson laid out Linton, Lindisfarne and Sybil Streets in 1881 and once this had been done a number of builders began to build on the land.

These included a Mr Wilson, who submitted plans for a total of eighty six houses, J. & N. Laing who obtained approval for sixteen houses in 1888, a Mr Metcalfe who built sixteen houses on Lindisfarne Street and a Mr. Beaty who obtained permission between 1889 and 1893 to build sixty more houses here.

St. Joseph's House (1892)
(Botcherby Home)

January 1892.

St Joseph's house was erected in 1892, as an institution of The Little Sisters of the Poor, who were established in Carlisle in 1880. It is situated near the village of Botcherby and can be seen across the River Petteril from The Linton Holme area. St Joseph housed about 110 aged poor of both sexes and was under the superintendence of the Rev. Mother.

Cumberland Directory 1934

Little Sisters of The Poor. No figures in the City are more familiar than those of "The little Sisters of the Poor" who in their simple dark robes move about in pairs. Unostentatiously carrying out their beneficent work for the benefit of the aged and destitute poor............

The architect's sketch plan for St.Joseph's Home, Botcherby

Their residence, St. Joseph's home stands high above the main road at Botcherby. Here in large, airy, and well lighted rooms, 14 sisters are at present in charge of 10 to 80 of the aged poor varying in age from 60 to 94, all more or less destitute and the majority of them so disabled by age and infirmity that self help is hardly possible. Without these Sisters, many of these inmates would not be able to claim a real friend in the wide world..............

The Sisters Duties.

.... up at 4.30 am. the sisters are hard at work till they are called to their beautiful chapel for mass at 7 am. Then comes their simple breakfast. By 10 am. the main work of the day is completed, though this does not include the personal care of the patients, the provision of dinner and other meals and the daily visits for the receipt of alms to the City and places farther afield.

A Few General Facts About The Home.

Through long rambling corridors and commodious rooms do not suggest it, the home is one of the smallest of 300 of it's kind scattered throughout the world.......... The movement began (1840) in a humble way by one who herself knew the meaning of being destitute. It is entirely dependent upon voluntary contributions, the order not even accepting in England the Government pensions to which the majority of inmates are entitled.

The only qualification for admission is age, (over 60) and destitution. Religion is no bar though no provision is made for religious service other than that of the Roman Catholic Church, attendance at this service is optional............

........Visitors are always made welcome by the Sisters and by the Patients..........   *Carlisle Journal,* **7 March 1924**

Some of the men from St. Joseph's Home, Botcherby, with their bottles of Christmas cheer which were presented to them by the Mayor during her visit on Christmas Day.

Carlisle Journal,
29 December 1967

1977 After 97 years in Carlisle the Little Sisters of the Poor gave notice of their intention to leave Botcherby Home. The reasons being *" a diminution of vocations and the necessity of having costly work carried out to the home, whose structure did not seem to justify it."* After several failed attempts to raise sufficient money to continue the home, the building was bought by the diocese and put onto the open market.

Portrait of a Parish, Our Lady and St Joseph's,
Kevin Rafferty

St Joseph's Home (1997) as seen from Melbourne Park

The Fire Engine House, London Road, (1894)

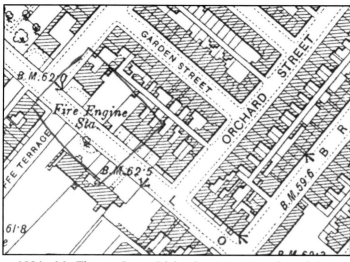

29 August 1866

The Carlisle Volunteer Fire Brigade (C.V.F.B.) was established, it was maintained by an annual grant from the corporation and by voluntary subscription. *Kelly's Directory - 1897*

A 5/- entrance fee for membership to the Brigade was introduced to both prevent "undesirables" participating and also raising capital.

In **1869** six manual engines were purchased by public subscriptions and allotted to suitable parts of the City.

In **1872** several additional hand engines were purchased and these too were located throughout the City, so there was no district in Carlisle without coverage .

The History and Development of Fire Fighting in the City of Carlisle 1800-1914, Steven Matthew's.

With the development of the Southern district of the City came the need for fire extinguishing appliances to be located in the vicinity. In 1894 a Mr. Thomas James Richardson gave over, free of charge, land situated in the garden of his home at 23. London Road (Today the area around the St. Nicholas Arms). The fire engine house was little more than a building in which to store the appliances.

23 March 1894

NEW FIRE STATION IN BOTCHERGATE - Last night a new fire station in connection with the Carlisle Volunteer Fire Brigade was opened in London Road , and in case of fire in the Botchergate district there can be no doubt that it will be of immense use . The station is situated in the garden adjoining Mr T.J.Richardson's house, near St Johns church, Mr Richardson who is a member of the Brigade, having given the site free of cost. Hitherto no fire extinguishing appliances have been kept in the southern portion of the city, the consequence being that in the event of an outbreak the hose reel on the West Walls has to be requisitioned. Now, however, a fully equipped hose cart, with 500 feet of hose, will be available in the district mentioned, and every member of the Brigade as well as the policemen on the London Road beat will have keys of the new fire station.

Last night members of the Brigade mustered in full force at their head quarters and marched down to the new station with the hose cart, which has been constructed by Messers. Atkinson and Davidson, while the apparatus it contains has been supplied by Mr. Coulthard, Castle Street. On their arrival at the Station Mr. Bell, captain of the brigade, handed Mr. Richardson a key with which he opened the new station, and the hose cart was then deposited therein. The chief constable (Mr Mackay) was present. Mr Richardson, in the course of a brief speech, expressed the hope that the hose cart would never be wanted but he added that he should always attend to it and keep it in order. *Carlisle Journal.*

31 December 1904

The C.V.F.B. was disbanded, the police were then in charge until a separate fire service was established in 1938.

In the 100 or so years since the establishment of a fire service in the city there have only been five fire chiefs; Captain J. Bell pictured below being the second of these. On the Whitsuntide Bank Holiday the service would have an annual outing, using the fire engine as a conveyance. The trip pictured below was from Carlisle to Brampton via Warwick Bridge, returning via Ruleholme and Crosby. If a fire occurred during one of these outings a policeman was detailed to ride by bicycle to find them and summon their assistance.

Jim Templeton, ex - fireman

Captain J Bell, Chief Officer of the Carlisle Volunteer Fire Brigade.

The Carlisle Volunteer Fire Brigade, circa 1875, at Low Gelt, near Brampton on a Whit Monday outing

Turn of the Century
(1899-1900)

As the beginning of the 20th century approached the local newspapers looked back at the achievements of mankind during the previous 100 years and it is interesting to observe how they viewed the undoubted progress that had been made.

" ....the distinguishing mark of the Century undoubtedly, is it's Science..... the Century was only a couple of years old when the Cumbrian John Dalton promulgated his Atomic Theory of the ultimate constitution of matter.............The labours of Farady and Brewster led up to electric telegraphy and that to the telephone and wireless telegraphy.

Carlisle and Cumberland

....A hundred year ago Carlisle was a pushing and prosperous town........We are apt to think that our situation as a railway centre and our modern improvements, have given Carlisle the new character of a desirable place of residence........In 1801 there would be old folk who well remembered Charles Edward's entrance to the City, his hurried retreat a few weeks later, the bloody assizes which ensued and the Rebel heads which 'adorned' the walls. With the collapse of the Stewart enterprise the importance of Carlisle as a Border Fortress appeared, but in a year or two manufacture of linens and woollens was started....In 1794 there were four printworks which employed a thousand hands, there were three breweries and a soap manufacturer............ The population which in 1801 numbered 9521 would thus be fully employed. ......An Act of Parliament was obtained in 1804 for lighting the streets and lanes with oil lamps, for paving footpaths and for making a road from English Street to Botchergate through the Citadel .... By another Act in 1807 the City walls were given to the County Justices for the purpose of erecting a new gaol and Courthouse. The fine bridge over the Eden, superseding two narrow dilapidated stone bridges was begun in 1812 and finished in 1815, at a cost of £70,000....... By 1815 a great change in the trade of Carlisle had taken place; it now consisted mainly in the manufacture of cotton goods........... There were eleven cotton mills, three printworks, besides dyeing and bleaching works, a small mill for weaving calicoes, a manufactory of carpets, three iron foundries and four public breweries......... In 1819 the canal to the Solway was made....... the opening of the canal, by bringing coal within easy reach paved the way for the establishment of the the gas works...... In 1829 the Christ Church (Botchergate) and the Trinity Church (Caldewgate) were built; and since the sixties we have added St. Pauls, St. Stephens, St. James and St. Johns..... The Waterworks ... a private concern were started in 1846 and were acquired by the corporation in 1865. Before 1846 the citizens obtained their supplies from wells or from the rivers..... In 1872 an Education Act was adopted."

Carlisle Journal, **28th December 1900**

1899 saw the laying of the foundation stone of St. Aidans Church by the Duchess of Devonshire and the erection of The Electric Lighting Station in James Street by John Laing Builders.

John Dalton of Eaglesfield, Cumbria, Founder of Atomic Theory

... In the review of the year now fast drawing to a close ..... For Englishmen 1899 will ever be memorable for the momentous struggle in South Africa.
Carlisle Journal, **29 December 1899.**

Yesterday was New Years Day and the beginning of the last year of the 19th Century. Most of the places of business in Carlisle were closed and with a fine sunny day to cheer the prospect, large numbers of people took outdoor exercise, while the usual excursions facillities on the Scottish lines were available. There were also excursions to London and other big towns in the south. The attractions in the City included "Variety" entertainment at Her Majesty's Theatre.
Carlisle Journal, **2 January 1900.**

Queen Victoria's Xmas message to the officers and men of the Army in South Africa is telegraphed from Capetown. Addressing the Generals Her Majesty says "I wish you and all my brave soldiers a Happy Christmas, God protect and Bless you all".....
Carlisle Patriot, **5 January 1900**

Left: St. Aidans Church seen here in 1901; the year in which the building was consecrated.

Gladys Harrison

Memories of Greystone Road in the early years of the century

Gladys, 102 years young (1998)

Gladys aged 10

At the time of writing Mrs Gladys Harrison, aged 103, is in excellent health and still lives in Greystone Road, not far from her father's shop, pictured below. The shop at 129 Greystone Road (originally 7 Nelson Terrace), occupied by William Charles Tait, was mentioned in the Carlisle directory of 1910, see page 49, but the family started trading there in 1898. Gladys has fond memories of those early days when there were very few houses around them. Builders started work nearby, constructing the first houses in Margery Street, and they came to the shop looking for pies etc., but at that time the shop did not have bakery goods. A friend of the family said that she would do some baking for them and told them to return later. From that day on they supplied bakery goods and every day her father would fill up two large baskets with cakes, pies etc. and tramp round the district selling them. He wouldn't eat one himself, just in case he could sell it, and he would return every day with empty baskets. Gladys says that he trekked out as far as Faugh at times, carrying his wares; an early mobile baker without a mechanical means of transport. Gladys also remembers the regular flooding that occurred from the River Petteril and how one of their neighbours was not above stealing sandbags from their property to protect his own. Gladys' mother continued trading at 129 Greystone Road, after her husband's death, until her own death in 1949. Other members of the family continued for a short time after that. Gladys was a pupil at Botcherby School until it was closed for three weeks because of an outbreak of the measles. Not wishing to miss out on her education she transferred to the Fawcett School on West Walls, a move she later regretted; because when Botcherby School was re-opened she could not transfer back. Gladys clearly remembers the old Greystone Cottages, see page 17, and seeing the inhabitants come out with their buckets to collect water from a single cold water tap. She also remembers 'Dick Death,' see page 21, and his two sons, Bill and Eric Irving who had the coalyard. Bill and Eric were inseparable, they were seen together every day and together in the pub every night, and they died within a week or so of each other. In her teens Gladys worked for a time at Bucks in Nelson Street, (the Atlas Works), and during World War 1 she worked at the NER Goods Yard at the Mains, but only for a few years. When the men returned from the war all the women got the sack. She remembers that some of the train crews stayed overnight at a cottage near the Goods yard in Tyne Street. This obviously preceeded the purpose built hostel, described on page 51. Gladys remembers that her mother had a three sided washhouse, open to the weather on one side. When Tulllie Street was being built her mother strung a washing line with a sheet up to hide the open side of the washhouse. She then pinched bricks from the building site and built up the fourth wall herself, under cover of the hanging sheet. The wall is probably still standing today. Gladys also recalls the sluice, the dam waterfall and 'the bay' on the River Petteril. Young boys would catch 'lampers' (eels) at the sluice, tie them together and hit the girls with them.

She recalls many of the occupants of the shop opposite to their own which frequently changed hands. This shop is recorded as 126 Greystone Road in the 1910 directory (see page 49). One owner called Thompson used to light the shop with candles because he came from the countryside. Another, Graham, of the Graham and Roberts family died only two weeks after taking over.

Another occupant called Stalker told Mr Tait he would see him out on the street (i.e. close him down through competition). However, when his business failed he asked Mr Tait to buy his stock. Around 1910 Mrs Wheatley had a fish shop at No. 126 and when she fell into debt she sold her piano and moved to a grocer's shop. Other occupants of the premises were called Tirrel, Babe, Trickett and R. Robinson; the last owner. Gladys also recalls Botcherby Mill Farm when it had a dairy herd and milk was sold using a gill (half pint) measure direct from the churns, which were carried round the streets.

Left: The Tait's shop at 129 Greystone Road, circa 1910

The Tram Sheds, London Road
(1899-1931)

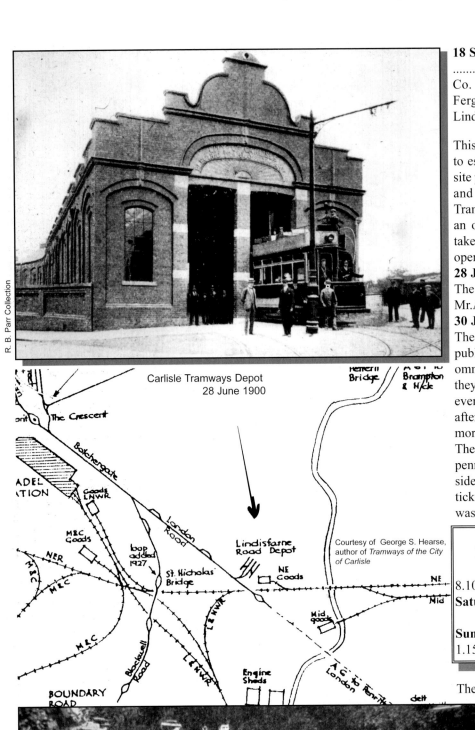

R. B. Parr Collection

Carlisle Tramways Depot
28 June 1900

Courtesy of George S. Hearse, author of *Tramways of the City of Carlisle*

Carlisle Journal

18 September 1899

........We hear that the Carlisle Tramways Co. have purchased from Mr. C. J. Ferguson, the site on the corner of Lindisfarne Street and London Road........

Carlisle Patriot.

This was, of course, the first practical step to establishing a tramway in Carlisle. The site purchased was to become the tramshed and maintenance depot for Carlisle Tramways. An inspection of a tramway by an officer of The Board of Trade had to take place before the system could be opened .

28 June 1900

The Carlisle tramways were inspected by Mr.A.P.Trotter of the Board of Trade .

30 June 1900

The Carlisle Tramway system opened for public service, replacing a service of horse omnibuses . The Company announced that they proposed to run cars on each section every 10 minutes on weekdays and Sunday afternoons, and every half hour on Sunday mornings.

The fares for each section would be one penny - for either travelling inside or outside the car. Each section had it's own ticket colour. The London Road section was purple.

Time Table
London Road to Citadel Station
8.10am and every 10 minutes to 9.50pm. **Saturday night only**, 10.50pm.
Sunday 9.45am and every half hour to 1.15pm then every 10 minutes to 9.50pm.

The London Road route left the Boundary Road line at the junction of London Road with Botchergate, a few yards into London Road was a loop. There were loops just before the depot on Lindisfarne Street and at the terminus just beyond the Railway bridge at London Road Terrace..........

Tramways of the City of Carlisle,
George S.Hearse.

Left: Before the introduction of the trams the people of Carlisle relied on the horse omnibus for public transport.
Here the Stanwix, Town Hall, Harraby horsebus is pictured in London Road, circa 1898.

The Tram Sheds, London Road
(continued)

Right: Inside the Tram Depot which was entered by two lines which had four roads in all, with inspection pits at the lower end, seen on **28 June 1900.**

Over the double entrance was a rising sun with the words City of Carlisle Electric Tramways Company.

Below: A Tram proceeds along London Road Towards the Tram Sheds in 1910

1906
The company began a parcel delivery service using Messenger boys, which proved to be more profitable than the trams.
24 September 1908.

Carlisle Trams were noted for being both slow and noisy. I am not sure how much this slowness had to do with one of the clauses in the Tramways Act of 1870, namely that: *The driver of every car shall cause the same to be driven at a speed of not less than four miles per hour and not exceeding 8 miles per hour.* Apparently a common saying in Carlisle was: *If you had plenty of time, catch a tram; if in a hurry, walk!*

Accident to a Farmer in London Road

A serious accident happened at Hill Top, Carlisle on Wednesday afternoon, to Mr Jeremiah Bainbridge, farmer, of Carleton. Mr Bainbridge had been to the City with a cartload of potatoes, and was returning home when his horse took fright at a tramcar, and turning round bolted. The driver was thrown down and a wheel passed over one of his legs, severely crushing it. He was carried into the Railway Hotel, and Dr. Hair, who was passing, found him to be suffering from shock, but with no bones broken. The injured man was then carried on a stretcher by two policemen and a Midland goods guard (Mr. Patrickson) to his sister's house in Aglionby Street. The horse in it's career knocked a wheel off the cart at the corner of Oswald Street, and proceeded with the remainder of the cart to the bottom of Grey Street, where it was caught by Thomas Green, coal agent , who took it to his own stables.

Carlisle Journal, **31 January 1902**

Left: A tram at the London Road terminus decorated for Princess Louise's visit on 24 September 1908

May 1910
The Company directors recommended that the shareholders should sell the undertaking as the company was in a serious state due to lack of custom and the high cost of electricity. The lack of maintenance of the track, overhead and the cars had led to their deterioration .

November 1911
Messrs. Balfour Beatty took control of the Company and having agreed on a reduction in the electricity costs were able to carry out extensive improvements costing in excess of £18000.

THE NEW TRAM CARS. - Good progress has now been made with the reconstruction of the tramway track in the city, and it is expected that the work will have been sufficiently advanced in the course of the next few weeks for the Company to start running the new cars before the end of the month. Some of them have already arrived in the city, and they are handsome modern vehicles............The colour scheme of the new cars is olive green and cream with gold lines, and there are wire guards round the railings on the top..........

Carlisle Journal, **4 October 1912**

The Tram Sheds, London Road
(continued)

Unfortunately even with this new investment, which included new wires, improved pylons, eight new double decker and four new single decker trams, the system continued to lose money. From 1908 motor buses introduced unwanted competition and by 1926 there were more than 40 bus operators in Carlisle. In December 1930 Ribble Motor Services agreed to take over the Tramway and replace the trams with motor buses. The city council was in favour of setting up its own municipal transport service and, in 1931, decided to purchase the Tramway and Percival Bus services for £32,500. They were frustrated in this by the Northern Transport Commissioners who, in June 1931, refused to allow the city to operate its own buses. This left the way open for Ribble to purchase the Tramway, which they then closed on November 21, 1931.   *Denis Perriam*

1926

Right: A Percival's Charabanc is standing outside Nos. 5-11 Brook Street. The competition from motor buses like this one, and the reputation of the tramway for being rather slow and antiquated, eventually led to the closure of the service.

**TRAMWAY DEPOT
To Become A Garage.**

The " Carlisle Journal " understands that the former Tramway Depot on London Road will shortly be opened as a garage operated by Messers. Stout's (Carlisle) ltd.
                    6 March 1936.

Above: The small boy standing at the fron of the bus is Tom Barlow; Lorraine's Grandfather

Handing over the keys - see text

THE PASSING OF THE TRAMS.
----o----
Saturday Night Excitement at the
Depot
" Auld Lang Syne "

The abolition of Carlisle's electric trams on Saturday was marked by exciting scenes in the streets.

Throughout the day the cars were well filled with passengers who were evidently satisfying their curiosity by having a last ride in the Carlisle trams.

Pressure on the accommodation was especially marked between 8 p.m. and 11.30. The return theatre cars, particularly the one from the Newtown district, was packed. People came out of their houses along the route from Newtown and cheered as the last car passed, and at the Tramway Depot in London road, where a crowd of several hundred people gathered, a scene of great excitement was witnessed, the arrival of the last car being greeted with prolonged cheering.

As soon as the car had been driven into the Depot the crowd sang "Auld Lang Syne."

Mr Sleight, the Tramway manager, handed over the keys of the Depot........ The work of removing the overhead wires along the various tramway routes has already commenced.

Carlisle Journal, **24 November 1931**

Left: A start was made yesterday in the removal of the tram-lines at London Road, preparatory to the reconstruction of the road. In the picture the men are seen lifting the lines at the London Road terminus, to which trams ran for thirty years.
Carlisle Journal, **21 February 1933**

John Laings, Builders

In **1874**, John Laing a stone mason from Sebergham came to Carlisle to start a building business. He bought plots of land in new streets, in the new developing suburbs of Carlisle, where he built rows of terraced houses. One such area was Lindisfarne Street where he began building in the late 1890's, becoming John Laing and Son by 1900. In order to handle the increase in the volume of work the firm had new offices and a yard built in Milbourne Street in 1904. John Laing had an 'out office' at the corner of Linton and Oswald streets, due to the extensive housing being built and let nearby. This was probably the firm's first branch office. John Laing was building houses at a cost of £150 - £175, which were let at 5 or 6 shillings (25 to 30p) a week.

Laing , The Biography of Sir John W. Laing , C.B.E., Roy Coad.

John Laing, 1842-1924

Left: John Laings bricklayers on a site near Carlisle , early 1920.

Right: Horse drawn transport was still familiar to the company in 1949, when this picture was taken.

It was John William Laing who moved the Head office to London in 1926, however John Laing Ltd. continued to build in the area. The corporation contracted them for Housing Schemes at Botcherby in 1928, Margaret Creighton Gardens in 1932 and Vasey Crescent in 1937. By the 1950's John Laing Ltd. was responsible for 7000 out of 14000 houses built in Carlisle.

February 1949.

Percy Dalton, The City Surveyor & Engineer for Carlisle, on his retirement in January 1949 wrote to John Laing., the letter was printed in the February issue of "Team Spirit" (A Monthly News sheet issued by J.Laing & Son Ltd.).

"................Between the two wars Carlisle at one time or another held various housing records, so I was informed at the Ministry of Health, Whitehall. This was only possible by your assistance and I shall always feel grateful for your firms co-operation in carrying out a work which must have contributed so much to the happiness of Carlisle Citizens..." *Percy Dalton..*

CONTRACTORS TO THE WAR OFFICE,
ADMIRALTY, AIR MINISTRY, OFFICE OF WORKS, &c.

JOHN LAING & SON,

Building & Engineering Contractors,

CARLISLE

Telephone 182

PLACE THEIR EXPERIENCE AND REPUTATION AT YOUR DISPOSAL AND WILL CAREFULLY ATTEND TO YOUR SMALLEST OR LARGEST REQUIREMENT.

John William Laing

45

Mildred Edwards

Childhood Memories of London Road around the turn of the Century

Mildred Edwards

"......On the right hand side of London Road after crossing Petteril Bridge heading into the City, were the Midland Railway Goods Sheds, a busy place for coal lorries and also lorries from Lings Mill (left side of London Road) with bags of flour and oatmeal. Next was the drive down a hill to Mains House and Weaving Mill by the River Petteril. The family at the house were called Wilson.

Then past the high wall of Harraby Hill, with hilltop houses on the left. This part was the old road to Penrith, before the main road was cut through the hill. Also on the Hill was the Gibbet where some of Prince Charles Army were hanged. I have heard it said, by an old builder that when excavations were being made to build on Summer Hill, the bodies of these men were found and the kilts and sporrans were all in good condition. This man also told me of the Roman remains which had been found........

After passing this part one came to the North Eastern Railway Goods and Engine sheds and the coal vaults where the Northumberland coal was brought We were always told to be careful crossing here as it was a busy place for lorries. Mrs Skelton's shop was at the corner of St. Cuthberts Street, the next shop was Mrs Murrays, fruit and veg, and everything else. Then next door was the Samson Inn, the Landlord was Ted Blair, he used to give us pennies for sweets. He would stand at the door passing a word with all who passed ...."
Edmund (Ted) Blair was the first manager of the Linton Holme Hotel (see page 72).

Right: The Samson Inn, being quite near to the London Road Station of the Newcastle and Carlisle Railway line, was named after one of the first locomotives to work the line.

"..........Houses ran along the way to the corner of Grey Street, here was a big house 'St Nicholas View' where the Miss Cartmels lived, three white haired ladies, who did much good work

in the City. On a winters evening one could see them working, sewing by the light of a yellow shaded lamp. At the entrance to the gate was a great Maple Tree, in Autumn the leaves were such a lovely colour, we children used to pick the leaves up off the pavement and press them between the pages of our prayer books. On the opposite corner was another big house, the Miss Dodds, two sisters, maiden ladies, the younger Miss Annie was a devout worker at St. Johns Church on the corner of Close Street.......

Our City ...Our People 1889-1978, memories by Mildred Edwards.

Miss Annie Dodds

The Petteril View Laundry (1902)

The Ordnance Survey map of 1925 shows a laundry situated next to the River Petteril, lying between Botcherby Mill and Raven Nook. Also known as Raven Nook Laundry, the premises were run by a Mrs Clegg. The laundry appears in the directories of 1902/8 through to 1913/14.

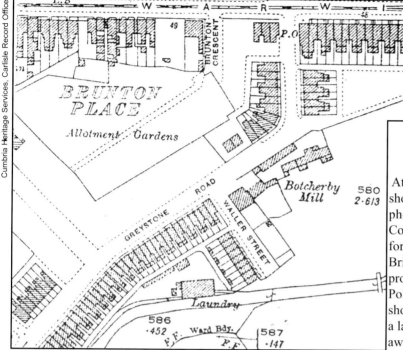

Cumbria Heritage Services, Carlisle Record Office

The mill race from the River Petteril ran through the laundry and the walls of this are still visible in the waste land between the site of the laundry and Raven Nook Mill.

Right: The left hand wall of the mill race which passes through Allen's scrapyard; formerly Mrs Clegg's laundry.

Left: Here the remains of the right hand mill race wall can be seen from the lane between Allen's scrapyard and Irving's Coaches

FIRE AT RAVEN NOOK
A Workshop Destroyed

At 12.40 on Tuesday morning fire broke out in a workshop at Raven Nook, occupied by Mr. Henry Smith, photographic Instrument Manufacturer. Police Constable Pattinson, who has only just joined the force, saw the flames as he was standing on Petteril Bridge, Warwick Road. He acted with commendable promptitude, blowing his whistle, he soon brought Police Constable Watson to the place, and in a very short time Mrs Clegg, Greystone Road, who carries on a laundry business in the same block of buildings, was awakened. The two constables also made their way into a stable adjoining the burning workshop and brought out two ponies in safety. Meanwhile the laundry had been cleared.......... In a short time the hose carts, with members of the Fire Brigade and police, under the command of the Chief Constable and Capt. Bell arrived. The fire was subdued by half past two O'Clock, but not before Mr. Smith's workshop with the whole of its contents had been gutted. The roof of the stable was also damaged slightly. The spread of the fire was only averted by the prompt action of the police and firemen, as some premises adjoined containing a huge quantity of inflammable material and Mr. Ridley's Petroleum Store was not far off. The total damage is put at £250. Mr Smith is insured up to £150, and the premises belong to Messrs. P. and J.W. Hayton, Land agents.

Carlisle Journal, **31 January 1902.**

Allen's Scrapyard - formerly Mrs Clegg's Laundry

Norman Street School (1908)

The plans for Norman Street Infants School for 400 children were approved in **March 1907**. The School was built for the Carlisle Education Committee on land of Greystone Road owned by the corporation. The plans were drawn up by architects George Dale Oliver and Edward J.Dodgshun, of Lowther Street. The estimated cost of building the School was £5,700, however by it's completion in 1908 and after going over budget, the actual cost of erecting and furnishing Norman Street School was £6,250.

Left: Organised games at Norman Street Infant's School   *(1924 Education Week pamphlet)*

The Norman Street School

.......the progress during the last few weeks has been poor owing mainly to the weather and to the holiday season. The walls of the school are now above the level of the window sills, glazed brick Dado's are now well advanced........the boundary walls have been built to enclose the site, and to keep the children off the ground. The playshed is ready for the slater. With better weather good progress ought now to be made.

The school management committee had requested the architects to submit an estimate for making all the floors level and for placing a blackboard surface on the walls opposite to the scholars.........

Carlisle Journal, **31 January 1908**

Norman Street School formally opened on **20 October 1908** although children were not admitted until 3 November. Almost all of the children attending St. Johns's Infant School entered the new school.

On inspection of the new school His Majesty's inspector described the school as a place where the conditions under which work is carried on are as near perfect as is possible to conceive them to be.

20 October 1908

At the opening ceremony the architect, Mr Oliver, gave a short description of the building, explaining that the whole work had been executed by local tradesmen: *"there had not been a single foreigner on the job, and he was thoroughly satisfied with everything that had been done."*

The School Board had purchased the site more than ten years before, mainly because of complaints due to overcrowding of the Brook Street Schools, but had failed to proceed with a new school. St. John's Infants School on South Street was opened in 1872 in a building which was originally a mission hall. The number of children on the roll then was 119, but in the course of time, owing to the successful way in which it was conducted and the growth of the population, the number of pupils more than doubled. Finally, when the South Street building was condemned, it was decided that St John's school would be closed and a new school for 400 infants would be built on the Norman Street site.   *Carlisle Journal.*

7 March 1952

A pleasant ceremony:- Children of Norman Street school on Tuesday planted twenty flowering trees, to mark the "de-requisitioning" of land adjoining the school which had been used as allotments throughout the war. It was part of a scheme mapped out by the Parent-Teachers Association to utilise school land as a garden. The Association will entirely finance the project which will, it is hoped result in the school having it's own garden with a pet's corner, a vegetable plot and, possibly an orchard. The garden will be used for nature studies and open air lessons. The trees were planted on each side of the main path to form an avenue......

Carlisle Journal

Shops in the District, (1910)

Lindisfarne Street.

82	James Winthorpe	Shopkeeper.
84	Robert Davidson	Bootmaker.

Oswald Street.

1	Mrs. Alice Scott	General Store.
2	George Tinn	General Store.
52	Mrs Mary Lancaster	General Store.

Brook Street.

1	William Bert Croxford	Fried Fish Shop.
29	Mrs. Mary Jane Melvin	General Shopkeeper.
72}	John Johnson	Joiner.
}	James Little	Clogger
100}	Ross Lawson	Grocer }Today's
102}	Town Sub Post Office.	} Cellar Five.

Sybil Street.

1	Mrs. Catherine Bell	Grocer.
2	Henry Etchells	General Shopkeeper.
6	Cameron & McGarr	General Shopkeeper.
9	Frederick Doidge	Butcher.

Greystone Road.

5	Joseph Emmerson	Blacksmith.
22	Mrs. Margaret Elliot	Milk Seller.
7a	Matthew Percival	Confectioner.
9 }	Joseph Henry Metcalfe	Hairdresser.
9a}	James Metcalfe	Butcher.
53	Mrs. Jessie Young	General Shopkeeper.

Corner of Jackson Street.

	Mrs. Lucy Armstrong	Confectioner.

Corner of Tullie Street. (formerly 7 Nelson Terrace).

	Charles William Tait	General Shopkeeper.
40	John Johnstone	Photographer (Upstairs)
}	Mrs. Francis Steel	General Shopkeeper (Below Stairs)
58	Miss. Clara Watson	Milliner.
120	James Davidson	General Shopkeeper.
122	Joseph Simpson	Boot Maker.
126	Mrs. Mary Wheatley	Fried Fish Shop.
206	William Ramsay Findlay	General Shopkeeper.

Brunton Avenue.

1	John Stalker	Grocer.
15	John Butler	Draughtsman.

Carlisle Directory.

The premises originally occupied by Ross Lawson's grocery shop and the town sub post office are now occupied by Cellar 5.

9a Greystone Road circa 1920. This small annexe to No. 9 is still in use as a shop today.

Photographer's Stamp (circa 1904)

Left: The Johnston family photographer's sign is still to be seen on the side of No. 40 Greystone Road. The photographer's studio window is on the second floor and Mrs. Steel's general store is seen below (now flats).

The Origins of the Allotment Society (1914)

The Home Food Culture Movement began in Carlisle after the outbreak of the first world war. A Committee was formed of local Landowners, Manufacturers and others who realised that the war would lead to unemployment. The problem being that, how workers on short time and reduced wages would manage without having to resort to charity.

Plenty of land was available and the landowners of the district were patriotic enough to lend their land free of rent and rates. The workers were keen to cultivate their small strips of land, and the horticultural experts of the County Council helped with advice and assistance.

In Carlisle there were 3 Allotment groups, Currock, Newtown and Greystone Road area. There was also a volunteer Corps. from the boys Grammar School who had a plot on land owned by The Duke of Devonshire on St. Aidans Road. There were even eight plots on waste land at Hudson Scotts.

Starting to fence off the area of land for the Greystone Allotment Society, **21 January 1915**

At Greystone Road a society of 35 members was formed to take over and work the land belonging to a Mr. Thompson, of Stanwix. The fencing materials were provided by the Home Culture Committee and the men erected the fences in their space. The plots were about 200 sq. yards. There only hindrance, being the weather.

Seeds of Changes .

Andrew Humphries & Newton Rigg Agricultural College.

September 1939. In September 1939, the number of allotments in the City was less than a quarter of those existing at the end of the World War 1, many of them having been used for council house building. In the south end of the city there were fewer than a dozen allotments and these were earmarked for sites for air raid shelters for children, with plans to put soil on the flat roofs and grow vegetables on top of them.......

Carlisle at War 1939-1940, David Hay.

A Horse and Cart carrying hops around 1910, here seen in the lane between Delagoa and Adelaide Street; next to the allotments.

Hostel for Trainmen of the N.E.Railway Co. Lindisfarne Street (1916)

A hostel for the Trainmen of the North Eastern Railway Co. was erected in late 1916, adjacent to the Linton Holme Hotel. It backed onto the Engine Sheds and so was conveniently positioned for its intended purpose. The hostel appeared to have been integrated well into the area until 1939 when its use had changed and complaints were raised about the behaviour of some of the residents.

ELEVATION TO STREET

The Building is still in use today as a hostel for men "of no fixed abode."

Methylated Spirit Drinkers in Lodging House Alleged

Criticism of the licensing of a lodging house in Lindisfarne Street, described as a " very respectable residential area " was expressed..... They said it was inhabited by methylated spirit drinkers, street singers and chanters who created a definite nuscience in the neighbourhood and that they knocked at the doors and begged while under the influence of drink, and when refused used obscene language.

People in that part of town don't want this lodging, it is a definitely respectable locality and the residents there have to keep their doors locked against these men.....They were not a desirable class of people, but since then there had been an improvement in the place.......

Carlisle Journal, **14th April 1939**

N. Routledge & Sons — *HIGH CLASS BAKERS AND CONFECTIONERS*
80 BROOK STREET, CARLISLE — Telephone 25656
BRANCHES: 46 DENTON STREET — 3 ST. ALBAN'S ROW — 45 BROAD STREET

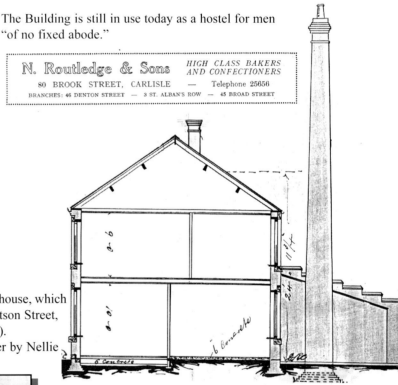

On the 20th July 1894 plans were proposed for a Bakehouse, which was duly built on the corner of Brook Street with Watson Street, for Mr George Rae, baker and confectioner (see right).
The bakehouse and shop that resulted were taken over by Nellie Routledge in 1917.

The business was continued in the same premises until 1946 when a further extension was built................

Above: Routledge's shop in Brook street today.
Left: John & Nellie Routledge, founders of Routledge's Bakers, with sons Donald and Douglas. John was the grandfather of Andy Routledge, who runs the business today.

51

Events around the District (1920's)

Right:
The Botcherby floods of **16 September 1918.** Looking across from Petteril Bridge, Warwick Road towards Botcherby Mill (centre background) and Greystone Road.

Mr. John Dixon, a regular in the "Lint" for over 50 years recalls :-
"In those days mainly large families lived in the area, I remember one family in particular, the McDermott's.
The McDermott men were particularly interested in Whippet Racing. These races would regularly take place on the Linton Holme, next to the River Petteril......."

Whippet Racing on The Holme

LINTON HOLME SPORTS
Boy's racing and Whippet Handicap

At the Linton Holme grounds on Saturday the programme consisted of a £15 whippet handicap and a 100 yards boys' handicap for prizes to the value of £10. Sixty boys ran in the handicap; and the dogs competing numbered 85. Some capital racing took place before a good attendance..........Whippet Handicaps will be held fortnightly.

Cumberland News, **23 October 1920.**

WHIPPET RACING
Linton Holme Society.

The Linton Holme Society held a members free dog handicap on Saturday, for which they gave the sum of £12 and a copper kettle. A large crowd assembled and some good racing was witnessed .The card comprised of 170 dogs made up into 29 heats. The semi final was keen and interesting, excitement marked the windup..........
Carlisle Journal, **5 April 1921.**

BIG CROWDS AT LINTON HOME
The largest crowd ever seen at a whippet handicap on the Linton Holme enclosure gathered on Saturday and Monday when 147 dogs competed for prizes to the value of £40.............

Carlisle Journal, **17 May 1921.**

Above: A group of owners waiting to race their dogs.

Left: Letting the dogs see the rag!

Showing a clean pair of heels to the rest of the field.

Left:To the right of the picture in the background is the Main Railway Bridge London Road.

Whippet racing at Linton Holme on 20 March 1923.   Photograph by R Joslin, Carlisle

July 1919   **Union Street Peace Celebrations**

There was obviously great rejoicing at the end of World War 1 and street parties were held throughout the city to welcome home the returning troops.

Templeton Collection

CITY OF CARLISLE

PEACE CELEBRATIONS

THURSDAY, the 18th SEPTEMBER, having been fixed for the CARLISLE PEACE CELEBRATIONS, the Mayor and Corporation trust that Employers of Labour and the Tradesmen of the City may see fit to close their works and places of business on that day, in order that their employees may have the opportunity of taking part in the proceedings, and those Citizens possessing Flags, Bunting, etc., are respectfully requested to decorate their premises in honour of the occasion.

A.H. Collingwood
Town Clerk.
Town Clerk's Office, Carlisle. 3rd September, 1919

Left: Here the celebrations in Union Street are well underway. Union Street was later to be renamed Rydal Street; when the houses were rebuilt as part of Carlisle's improvement programme in later years.

Botcherby Airstrip (1920 - 1924)

Saturday 2nd. February 1920 In the early 1920's Botcherby had its own airstrip, the first officially recognised Civil Aerodrome in the region, and entrepreneurs were quick to exploit the interest of the local population in flying for excitement and pleasure. Not only could one fly, or watch a display but one could also go to the local cinema and see film taken of the events of the previous day.
17 February 1920

THE CARLISLE JOURNAL, TUESDAY, FE

The PICTURE HOUSE,
Daily from 2.30.   BOTCHERGATE   Saturdays 1 to 10.30

TO-DAY, & Daily During Flying :
CARLISLE'S AVIATION CARNIVAL.

Exclusive pictures taken Day by Day by special arrangement. Films taken one day are Screened Following Evening.

Cumberland News

SUCCESS OF CARLISLE AIR CARNIVAL.

Extension of the Original Period.

The Oldest Lady Passenger Carried.

Portrait of Mrs. Lowthian ready to Ascend.

Following the success of the Aviation Carnival the organisers decided to set up their own company to provide pleasure flights.

15 May 1920 The Cumberland News reported that a local *"Border Aviation Company"* had been formed to promote pleasure flying in the district. The company had purchased the latest type of three seater Avro machine with a 110 horsepower Le Rhone engine. Captain Hudson would be flying with it from Manchester with Captain Oliver and a mechanic this afternoon (Friday)...... Pleasure flights would cost one guinea for a ten minute trip.... Special flights and exhibition flights could be arranged.

Photo   "Carlisle Journal"

Peter Connon

Epilogue: After a series of plane crashes the Company faced financial difficulties and ceased trading on **21 October 1920.**

Botcherby Airfield with St Joseph's Home in the background. Captain Oliver is second from the left.

St Nicholas Arms, London Road (1921)

St Nicholas Arms (April 1999)

The House known a "St. Nicholas View" (see Mildred Edwards, page 45) was built for Mr Isaac Cartmel (an ex-City treasurer) in **1822/3.** It became the St. Nicholas Arms in **1921** when it was opened as a Public House under the State Management in order to deal with overcrowding in the existing ale houses.

LIQUOR CONTROL BOARD

Meeting of the Local Advisory Committee ST NICHOLAS VIEW

The Committee decided to commence alterations to give more floor space at the Crown and Cumberland, Botchergate so as to enable the Hare and Hound, Botchergate to be closed temporarily on the opening of St Nicholas View.

Carlisle Journal, **21 July 1921.**

".....the board purchased it and have turned it into a very fine public house. The plot in front has been preserved and laid with crazy stone work. Large trees have been left standing, making the approach to the house very pleasant.......the place is a pleasant, comfortable and orderly house."

St. Nicholas Arms Records, Carlisle Library

However there was diquiet within a section of the population at the number of alehouses in Carlisle.

14 October 1922

"...No meals are provided in the lately newly licensed and furnished St. Nicholas Arms....We counted sixty five men, most of them young enter the St. Nicholas in twenty minutes.." *Drink Nationalization in England and it's Results 1927*

Observations by Stuart Wilson.

A distinguishing feature of the St. Nicholas Arms is the large London Plane tree in the front garden which is the subject of a preservation order. Renovations costing £3840 took place in 1968/9 after many complaints, including a petition from customers about " ....the heating arrangements and the poor decorative condition of the house...."

The St. Nicholas Arms was amongst the 170 pubs, hotels, restaurants and off sales to be sold to private enterprise after the abolition of Carlisle and District State Management Bill of May 1971. The premises were acquired by John Smiths Brewery in May 1973. In 1983 Pat Cody took over "The Grand Old City Pub in the Doldrums" and in 1985 extensive refurbishments were undertaken for Matthew Brown Brewery at a cost of around £50,000. Mildred Edwards (page46) said the tree in the front garden was a Maple tree. This was a subject for argument in the pub and the local press until, in 1986, experts from the British Museum confirmed that the tree is in fact a London Plane; one of several planted in the area, possibly when the house was built in the 1820s.

Pub game boost for old folk

CUMBRIA'S old folk were winners at the St. Nicholas Arms, Carlisle.

Staff and customers of the London Road pub raised a magnificent £422 for the News and Star Old Folks Appeal — mainly from a charity football match.

News and Star editor Vernon Addison received the cheque on behalf of the appeal from Diane Cody. They are pictured above with some of the footballers.

Mr Addison said: "This is the second year the St. Nicholas Arms has supported our appeal, and once more they have made a tremendous effort that is much appreciated.

"And I am sure the old people of the county also appreciate the concern and care shown by everyone involved in raising the amount."

St Nicholas Arms patrons taking part in a charity football match in aid of the Evening News and Star Old Folks Appeal in 1986.

Robertson's Bakers & Confectioners (1922)

A fleet of vans drove into the city one morning 65 years ago (1936) and changed the locals eating habits....The city was Carlisle and inside each vehicle was a consignment of the baking world's latest "miracle" -

Sliced Bread.

The public bought the attractively packaged bread, tasted and came back for more. The local bakers protested to an unsympathetic public that the bread came from Gateshead. They sent vehicles and men through the streets carrying banners claiming : Carlisle bread for Carlisle people? But still the demand for the new sliced bread was here to stay. Only the enterprising and adaptable survived.

Above: delivery vehicles outside the Watson Street Bakery in the 1930s and, below, in the 1920s

Foremost among these bakers was a baker from Fife; William Cruckshank Robertson. He had taken over an existing business consisting of a small bakehouse and shop in Watson Street with it's back entrance onto Lindisfarne Street (today flats) and a shop at 78 Brook Street in 1922 and borrowed £100 from a great aunt in Scotland to buy his first mixer, belt driven by a petrol engine.... The Denton Street shop was opened 2 years later, followed by one on Warwick Road. There was a small shop in Caldewgate in the early 1920's, but it was closed after a short time. He tried unsuccessfully to introduce hand sliced bread to Carlisle in 1934 . It was a laborious and time consuming task and the public didn't respond sufficiently to make it worth while. However, the introduction of a bread slicing machine by the Americans eventually changed everything. Apart from the rival Gateshead firm there was only one other baker with such a machine. He was at Preston. The enthusiastic William Robertson was quick off the mark. While others faltered he arranged for thousands of sliced wrapped loaves to be delivered from Preston in time for opening in the morning. The rugged Morris 10cwt. vans struggling over Shap during the night became a familiar scene between Preston and Carlisle. Equally familiar was the number of half shafts they broke on the way, due to overloading as much as road conditions. Furniture vans were brought in and the loaves packed in like bricks. One way or another they battled up Shap and through blizzard conditions which often prevailed. In the morning an unsuspecting but appreciative public bought the freshly delivered loaves in their thousands. It was British initiative at it's best and it paid off, Robertson's not only survived but it flourished........ William Robertson was the first in Carlisle to put horse drawn bakery rounds on the road in the 1920's. By the 1930's petrol driven vehicles had been introduced and Robertson's also began supplying grocers shops as well as bakers, Robertson's now had more bakery rounds on the road than anyone else..........They became the major bakery company of the Carr's Milling Industries Group in 1956...... Extracts from *"A slice of the future"* in 1936, *Cumberland News*, **10 July 1981.**

The Bakery of 1922 remained at Watson Street until 1958 at which time the main plant was moved to the present site at Durranhill .....

Mr William Cruickshank Robertson retired in 1953, with his son Iain Robertson taking over the business. Mr Robertson retired to Bournemouth, he returned to Carlisle 6 months prior to his death on Sunday 2 June 1974, aged 81.

Today Robertson's Limited, with over 75 years experience in the bakery industry, have grown to be brand leaders throughout Cumbria and the Borders... Deliveries are made of daily fresh bakery products to

ROBERTSONS,
Wholesale and Retail
Bakers & Confectioners.

Famous for their quality products, Messrs Robertson's provide the daily bread for hundreds of families in this part of the County.......

........Many people in the Carlisle district have appreciated the bread, cakes and confectionery of Messrs Robertson's, and so the business has grown.....The firm's Watson Street Bakery is a monument to progress ; it is a good example of hygienic care and fully equipped with the latest and most efficient machinery and appliances........

Cumberland News, **17 September 1938.**

The LOAF you'll Love!

Robertson's **FOURPIECE** LOAF -- The nearest approach to pre-war white bread. Obtainable at Most Local Grocers

Supplied sliced and wrapped if desired

If unable to obtain please phone Carlisle 976

W. C. ROBERTSON (Carlisle) **Ltd.**
Watson Street Bakery, Carlisle

Left: an electric delivery vehicle from the 1950s outside the Watson Street Bakery.

Strathclyde and Grampian in the North and Tyneside, Teeside, Yorkshire and Lancashire to the south.........

Robertson's Ltd Promotional Leaflet .

Events in the district (1925-28)

Floods were a recurring problem in the 1920's

2 January 1925

Left: The Botcherby bus making it's way along Warwick Road. The Star Inn can be seen to the right of the background.

Below: In the floods of September 1926 cattle were herded to safety along Warwick Road near Botcherby.

21 September 1926

THE EAST END OF THE CITY.

During the early hours of Friday Morning a rapid rise of the River Petteril caused an extensive flooding of the lower end of Warwick Road. The stretch of road from Warwick Place to the Star Inn, Botcherby was covered by a swirling torrent which completely inundated the grounds of St. Joseph's home and neighbouring fields
Carlisle Journal, **6 January 1925.**

August/September 1928   Below: A view from Petteril Bridge, looking towards the Railway

Below::
Warwick Road flooded near the Star Inn

In 1925 the new "Brunton Building Estate" was commenced, between Greystone Road and Warwick Road, with fine looking semi-detached houses being offered for sale.

Then, in 1927, the corporation acquired some 11,063 acre of land from Mr. Martin Casey.

The north west corner of the Estate was placed at the disposal of the Parks Committee for use as a public playing field.

The south side was let to the Education Committee for use as school playing fields. The land to the rear of Raven Street and extending towards Warwick Road became known as "Graystone Park" and to the south "Melbourne Park" in 1928.

Councillor, Mr. Borland expressed a worry about the supervision of the children playing in the park, names were submitted of local residents who were prepared to act as volunteer Park Constables to maintain proper order and protection for youngsters using the playing fields.

Botcherby Housing Estate (1928)

After the purchase of land from Mr. Casey in 1927 for the use as playing fields, the remainder of the land was to be utilised for the erection of dwelling Houses These houses became known as the Botcherby Housing Estate.

The City Engineer and Surveyor responsible for the scheme was Mr. Percy Dalton.

Building began on phase one of the scheme in 1928 with additional dwellings being built into the 1930's. Three main building firms were involved in the scheme (see the extract from the Council Minutes, 1928, below).

1928 The Depression and Unemployment

Unemployment was a great problem at this time and a Special Unemployment Committee was set up to formulate schemes of work in the city. One of these was a plan for the construction of a raised footpath from Botcherby Avenue to Melbourne Road, together with an estimate of the cost amounting to the sum of £1,500. It was resolved that the Town Clerk, Frederick G. Webster be requested to apply to the Ministry of Health to borrow the money for the work.

21 February 1925

BRUNTON BUILDING ESTATE.
(OFF WARWICK ROAD).

Pair of Houses completed—Brunton Avenue.

This Popular Building Estate is now being quickly built up. The **SECOND BATCH** of **HOUSES** are nearing completion, and the **THIRD BATCH** is in course of erection. There are only one or two sites left in **BRUNTON AVENUE**, and if you wish to secure a **COMFORTABLE**, well-built **BRICK HOUSE** consult E. J. HILL, who has built houses in Carlisle and District for over a **QUARTER OF A CENTURY.**
The **BRICK BUILT HOUSE** is still declared by all shades of opinion the **Most Comfortable, Most Durable**, and it has stood the **TEST OF TIME.**
You can become **OWNER** of your **OWN HOUSE** by paying a small deposit and about '7s 0d **PER WEEK as Rent**, also obtain the assistance of the £100 **SUBSIDY** granted by the Carlisle Corporation.
E. J. HILL is in a position to supply these **BRICK HOUSES** now and without delay.

Property Repairs of every description promptly attended to by practical and efficient workmen.

E. J. HILL, THE BUILDER.
TEL. 311. **ST. NICHOLAS, CARLISLE.**

Cumberland News

Botcherby Estate.

Cost of 16 Non-parlour and three-bedroom houses (J. & R. Bell, Ltd.)	£4,853	9	4
Cost of 22 Parlour and three-bedroom houses (J. Laing & Son, Ltd.)........	8,431	6	4
Cost of 44 Non-parlour and two-bedroom houses (J. Laing & Son, Ltd.)	12,555	2	0
Cost of 32 Non-parlour and three-bedroom houses (Border Engineering Contractors, Ltd.)	9,888	0	0
Allowances for Contingencies, Clerk of Works Wages, Architectural Assistants' Salaries, &c.	893	2	4
Street Works	5,358	0	0
	£41,979	0	0
Total	£109,361	0	0

Carlisle Journal

Right: Work in progress on the Corporation's Housing scheme at Botcherby (1928).

The River Petteril (1929 - 1932)

12 November 1929

This photograph from the Carlisle Journal illustrates quite well the severe flooding problems which plagued the area in the early part of this century. The Star Inn, on the corner of Victoria Road (now a guest house) can be seen in the background to the right.

With all the new housing that was being erected a solution had to be found to prevent the regular flooding of the Petteril Bridge area of the city. In addition there was a continuing need to address unemployment in the city by providing suitable civil improvement projects to occupy those out of work as a result of the industrial depression.

22 December 1930.

The City Surveyor, Mr Percy Dalton, submitted a scheme for diverting the course of the River Petteril behind Greystone Road with a view to alleviate flooding and providing work for the relief of unemployment.

Going home by rail! A Botcherby resident's attempt to get home dryshod in the floods.

Council Minutes 1931, Cumbria Heritage Services,
Record Office, Carlisle.

It was decided that this work would go ahead after the City Road Improvements of Warwick Road Bridge were completed. However once again the area was the scene of great floods proving that the work on the River Petteril could be put off no longer.

FLOODS AFTER THE STORM
Botcherby scene reminiscent of the 1902 floods

The Eden and The Petteril rose rapidly during the night .Water reached almost up to the top doorstep of the Star Inn at Botcherby .

Petteril Bridge and The Star Inn were submerged to a depth of nearly two feet .

As in 1902, that portion of Warwick Road and Petteril Bridge was also under water the level was up to the doorsteps of many houses . Greystone Road and adjacent Streets were also affected, and Brunton Place, on the main Road, came inside the area of submersion, the advancing water all coming from the Petteril side of the Road. The rush of water was a thrilling sight.

People living in Greystone Road were unable to proceed to their work on Monday Morning.

Cumberland News, **20 June 1931.**

Vehicles splashing along the flooded roadway near Botcherby road-end, which was considerably flooded after the torrential rains at the weekend. The scene at Botcherby was reminiscent of the great flood of 1902.

11 August 1931

Above and left: Workmen altering the course of the River Petteril in order to prevent flooding on the Warwick Road.

The scheme was obviously effective as on **28 October 1932** the *Carlisle Journal* reported on recent flooding:

FOUR INCHES OF RAIN - October likely to prove the wettest month.... Last Friday provided the biggest deluge..........the Petteril also rose ....some of the junior football pitches in the Botcherby area were under water........and matches had to be cancelled on Saturday..........there was no flooding of roads or houses in the Warwick Road vicinity, which was probably due to the reconstruction of Petteril Bridge and the rivers course at that point

Petteril Bridge, Warwick Road, widening (1931) & Margaret Creighton Gardens (1932)

The road improvements mentioned on the previous page included the widening of the Petteril Bridge which, with increasing vehicular traffic, was proving to be a bottleneck as can be seen in the photograph on the right; published in the *Carlisle Journal* on **13 December 1929**. The amount by which the road was widened is illustrated in the photograph below which shows the improvements being carried out. The original footpath and gas lamp have yet to be moved. Apart from the widening and the changes in street furniture the view is much the same as it appears today, 70 years on. Other improvements included raising the level of the road to further reduce the chance of flooding.

The old and the new road levels at Botcherby can be seen in the *Journal* photograph showing the bus, of **9 October 1931**. In spite of this floods were still a problem in **1932**; see the news article below.

Margaret Creighton Gardens, Friday 11th. November 1932.

THUNDERSTORMS
SERIOUS FLOODING IN CARLISLE

ANXIOUS NIGHT IN WARWICK ROAD DISTRICT.

Residents near Petteril Bridge and in Greystone Road had an anxious night. The River Petteril was slow in rising but by midnight, Sunday a considerable expanse of land between Greystone and Botcherby was flooded.

The water rushed around by Raven Street onto Greystone Road with great force completely flooding Botcherby Mill Diary, occupied by Mr. and Mrs. Johnston and their family, who were marooned on the farm.............

.............The footpath on both sides of Warwick Road near the River Petteril was flooded over........

...........Houses in Brunton Avenue had their gardens submerged and allotment gardens at Greystone were flooded........

Carlisle Journal, ...June **1932**

Margaret Creighton Gardens were built on the 3¼ acres, formerly known as *"Old Greystone"*.

The land had been acquired by the corporation for the sum of £1100, and the scheme to build adequate and suitable accommodation for the aged people of the City began in March 1932.

Margaret Creighton Gardens (continued)

The contractors for the job were Messrs. John Laing and Son ltd., under the supervision of the City Engineer and Surveyor, Mr Percy Dalton, who described the scheme as follows:

The number of dwellings for the aged provided was 64.... the blocks are grouped around a rectangular grass courtyard being entered by a tree lined avenue......Interest in the scheme has been manifested by Corporations as far apart as Aberdeen and Wales,.....

Tenants were selected by the Finance Sub (Estates) Committee. Applicants were invited from interested aged persons, all information was given except the names of applicants or any details which would lead to their identification.

In the centre of the gardens there was a reading and recreation room for the inhabitants.

COTTAGES TO LET AT A RENT OF 4s. 4d. A WEEK.

An experiment in housing was carried out yesterday at Carlisle by the opening of 64 cottages to be let at 4s. 4d. a week rent, inclusive of electric lighting, to tenants between the ages of 60 and 90. The total cost per cottage, including land, sewering and roads, was £195 8s. 6d.

Carlisle Journal, **11 November 1932**

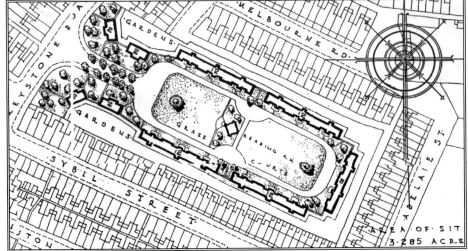

An original plan showing the layout of the gardens when first built

The dwellings were named after the late Mrs. Margaret RS Creighton, wife of twice Mayor Mr. Archibald Creighton. At the time of her death aged 52 years old on Wednesday 3rd. October 1932, they were living at No. 9 St. Aidens Road. Mrs Creighton took an active interest during her lifetime in the social welfare of the City.

AN APPRECIATION

An old friend of Mrs. Creighton contributes the following appreciation :-
There has passed away one who will long be remembered in religious, political, and temperance circles in Carlisle and Cumberland. It is but commonplace to say that she was indefatigable. Her energy was unceasing. At Charlotte Street Church she was in the forefront in all manner of services, with Girl Guides, ladies sewing meetings, indeed in every part of the church work she was found helping. As hostess to visiting preachers she was a perfect lady of the house.
She served a time as Chairman of the congregational Union of Cumberland, and visited, I believe, nearly every church in the county during her term of office. Her visit to the United States in connection with the celebrations of commemoration of the landing of the Pilgrim Fathers was inspiring, and on her return she lectured at several of our Congregational churches on her visit.

Mrs Margaret Creighton, Twice Mayoress of Carlisle

Mrs Creighton was a valued member in the British Women's Temperance Movement whilst in the Liberal Party she seemed indispensable. For some years she was secretary of the Carlisle Women's Liberal Association, and during her husband's candidature of the City she was an able seconder. She spoke at all his meetings, and threw herself into the contest as she did in other work - with an enthusiasm which was always infectious. But she was in truth not only a wife and helpmate; she was an equal partner in most of the labours of her husband. Mrs. Creighton was Mayoress on two occasions, and she never seemed to tire. She enjoyed helping others. One of her many little acts of kindness lay in conveying sick folk to and from Silloth in her car. She will be long remembered, not only for her important work, but for the little acts of kindness which were only known by the recipients.

Carlisle Journal

OFF TO SILLOTH- A photograph taken at Margaret Creighton Gardens Yesterday, when members of the Rotary Club of Carlisle took old-age pensioners on an outing to Silloth. *Carlisle Journal, 20 May 1949.*

Carlisle Journal, **6 August 1932**

Events around the District (1930s)

Friday 14th. September 1923

The need to acquire land for new housing schemes was increasing at this time and at a special meeting of the Housing and Development Committee it was resolved:

"That in accordance with the provisions of section 163 of the local Government act, 1933, the Town Clerk be requested to make application for the approval of the Ministry of Health to the appropriation of approximately 3.88 acres of land situate between Margery Street and Halfeys Lane, and used as Allotments, for housing purposes under the Housing Acts of 1925 -1935. This was the end of the Fusehill Allotments and the beginning of the development of Vasey Crescent.

Council Estate In Crescent Design.

Vasey Crescent a new group of council houses erected in the Greystone Road District. (Vasey Crescent was built by Laing's).

John Laing and Son. Carlisle.

..........In the Carlisle area the home of this Firm, beautifully selected sites have been obtained in healthy neighbourhoods for houses which are built to suit every class of House Purchaser.

Carlisle Journal, **12 March 1937**

The Coronation Year, Saturday 15 May 1937

STREET PARTIES

Joy Day for Thousands of Children.

There was no abatement of Coronation enthusiasm in Carlisle on Thursday when many hundreds of children and grown ups in various streets held their tea parties. A *Cumberland News* representative who visited a number of these gatherings, found smiling children and their parents seated at tables laden with good things such as Salmon and Ham sandwiches, fancy cakes, jellies, cream trifles and other delicacies..........

Brook Street. The children of Brook Street had a most enjoyable time through the efforts of Mr and Mrs. Robertson, Mrs K.Loughran and Mrs Horan, who had collected a good sum of money Each child received a souvenir and the adults had tea in the evening. The children indulged in sports and games after tea.

Sybil Street and Sebergham Terrace.

Sybil Street had been artistically decorated for the Street party, and Mesdames, Carruthers, Davidson, Ashbridge, Goody (Secretary), McPherson (Housekeeper at the Linton Holme Hotel), Bell and Henderson had provided an excellent repast, to which the children did full justice. Sports were held in the evening, followed by a dance in the Norman Street School. Coronation Souvenirs were presented to each child ,also sweets and fruit.

Raven Street and Melbourne Road.

Thirty eight children in the Raven Street and Melbourne Road districts thoroughly enjoyed their Coronation tea in the open air which had been arranged by Mr. and Mrs Hodgson and Mr. and Mrs T W Smith. Clad in Union Jack hats, they did ample justice to the good things which had been provided. The younger boys received a beaker and a ball, and the older ones knives and handkerchiefs. The younger girls received fountain pens and handkerchiefs, and the older girls Coronation Bangles and

The Coronation party at Borland Avenue, Botcherby

handkerchiefs. These were presented by Mrs. Cockburn, the oldest inhabitant of Raven Street. In the evening the children were taken to Silloth and Allonby.

Botcherby Avenue.

Assembling at the end of the Avenue the children marched down to St Aidens Mission Hall where they had tea, games and dancing, each child received a souvenir, In the evening the parents had a supper and dance . Billy Blythe's Band supplying the music.........

Cumberland News.

Left:*Cumberland News*
12 May 1937

61

Shops in the district (1938)

Ronnie Chandeler aged 67 years old has been a regular at the Linton Holme Hotel for forty nine years.

He has been cleaning the windows around the area since the age of fourteen as did his father and grandfather before him.

Ronnie recalls as a young boy during the 1930's playing around *"The Lint,"* the area opposite was wasteland (Now flats); this was where the local bonfires were held.

Ronnie says he has seen many changes in *"The Lint"* and in the surrounding area. He recalls the disappearance of all but a handful of shops since that time.

In 1938 the following shops were listed in the Carlisle Directory, for the Linton Holme area.

Lindisfarne Street

84	James Stanley Carruthers	Boot Repairer

Sybil Street

52	Mrs. Elizabeth Burton	General Shopkeeper
53	George Tinn	General Shopkeeper

Brook Street

49	Charles Dalziel	Pharmacist
78	William C. Robertson	Confectioners
80	Mrs Nellie Routledge	Confectioners
100	{Issac Styth	General
	Shopkeeper.	
102	{Brook Street Stores.	

Greystone Road.

7a	J.Mackintosh	Fishmonger
9a	W.Hodgson	Butcher
53	John Bowron	General Shopkeeper
40	Alfred Johnston	Photographer
40a	Mrs Annie Johnston	General Shopkeeper
111	William H.Irving	Upholsterer
127	Harold Trickett	General Shopkeeper
129	Mrs Annie Tait	General Shopkeeper
100	Charles Davidson	Millwright.
126	Albert Hoggard	Fried Fish Shop
206	John Martin	Grocer.

Tullie Street.

1	William N.Cameron	Grocer
9	Mrs Georgina Woodhouse	Baker
11	Mrs Mary Wilson	Confectioner
6	John H.Simpson	Butcher

Ronnie also remembers that all of the children called the pillar at the hotel entrance *"the potted meat post,"* due to its appearance (see picture on page 94). He still uses the nickname today. During World War II the wasteland opposite *"The Lint"* (now flats) was the site of an underground air raid shelter for the people of the area. It later became a garage owned by a man called Tommy.

Above:Charles Dalziel the Pharmacist also offered Optician's Services

A typical shopping list from around 1938.

1 lb. Bacon	1s.8d.
3 lb. Joint of Beef	1s.4d.
12 Eggs	1s. 6d.
1 lb. Butter	1s. 5d.
1 lb. Carrots	2d.
Cauliflour	5d.

For the benefit of younger readers: in 1938 there were 240 old pence (d), and 20 shillings (s) to the £1. Therefore 1 shilling, 12 old pence, was equivalent to 5 new pence.

The 1940s, Carlisle United & Ivor Broadis

Carlisle United was born in 1904. In May there had been a meeting of the shareholders of Shaddongate United and a vote was carried to change the name to *Carlisle United.* The team moved to Devonshire Park, (now the site of Newman School) in 1905. The first match at the present Brunton Park ground was on 2 September 1909 and the ground was purchased as a football ground in 1922.

During World War 2 Ivor Broadis was stationed near Carlisle and began to play for them regularly in the northern section of the wartime league. In 1946 Ivor became Player/Manager for Carlisle United; the youngest ever at the age of 23 years old. He lodged at **215 Greystone Road** and stayed with Carlisle until 1949. Ivor's wedding to a Carlisle girl at St Aidan's Church in June 1948 caused great excitement in the city, particularly amongst the womenfolk. Soon after, in 1949, Ivor Broadis negotiated his own transfer to Sunderland (for an £18000 fee). He later played for Manchester City, Newcastle United, and England.

Carlisle Journal

Part of the crowd outside St. Aidan's Church for the wedding of Mr. Ivor Broadis and Miss Joan Hendrie

Ivor was very successful as an international player, winning no less than 14 England caps before returning as Player/Coach for Carlisle in 1955.

Ivor Broadis Picked For England
Surprise Selection Catches the Critics Napping
A BOLT FROM THE BLUE-ON WASHING DAY, TOO!

"Everything happens on washing day !" declared a Carlisle housewife yesterday - but nothing quite like this had happened in Carlisle before.

Not only was it washing day, but the little Burgh Road bungalow was in process of being dismantled for their impending removal to Manchester, and then they had a caller.

The caller was a Carlisle City policeman, the housewife was Mrs. Ivor Broadis, the charming young wife of Carlisle's former football idol, now with ...ter City, and the news was that he had been picked for England.

... good news out of the blue, Ivor left for London yesterday after-... Wednesday in what had already been termed ...the England team,

Ivor Broadis stayed with Carlisle until the Summer of 1959. He then went to play for Queen of the South for two years until his retirement from football in 1961.

Ivor still kept in contact with the sport however by starting a new career as a sports reporter for the Newcastle Journal and Sunday Sun

Ivor Broadis

Ivor and Family at home in 1955

He remained with the Journal for seventeen years and during this time, in 1966, he was again involved with the World Cup; this time to report on the event rather than to play in it.

In 1977 Ivor returned to Carlisle as a sports reporter for the Evening News. He retired from his full time job in 1987 but still continued to write a football column until the 1999 season.

Ivor's son, Mike Broadis is carrying on in his father's footsteps. He is a freelance reporter, whose business is the Carlisle Newsagency

Carlisle United Football Club 1956 - 1957

| ...ck: | Hill, | Forbes, | | Fairley, | Thompson, | Kenny, | Waters |
| ...ont: | | Mooney, | Broadis, | Ackerman, | | Garvie, | Bond |

Ivor in 1999

Adelaide Street Kitchen Dining Room (1951)

For many decades parts of the land lying next to the River Petteril were used as refuse tips The land on which the Adelaide Kitchen Dining Room (K.D.R.) was constructed was one such area. Prior to the K.D.R being built the area was used as allotments and for pigeon lofts for housing the pigeons of The Linton Holme Flying Club; dating back to the 1920's.

Central kitchens for the preparation of school meals were the norm in the first half of the 20th Century.

In 1951 concern was expressed by the Ministry of Education at the high cost of running the existing establishments, because of a decrease in the take up of school meals, which gave rise to underuse of the facility and consequent overstaffing. It was decided to close the Petteril Central Kitchen, South Henry Street (sometimes referred to as The Mart Billiard Hall) and The Wetheral Kitchen.

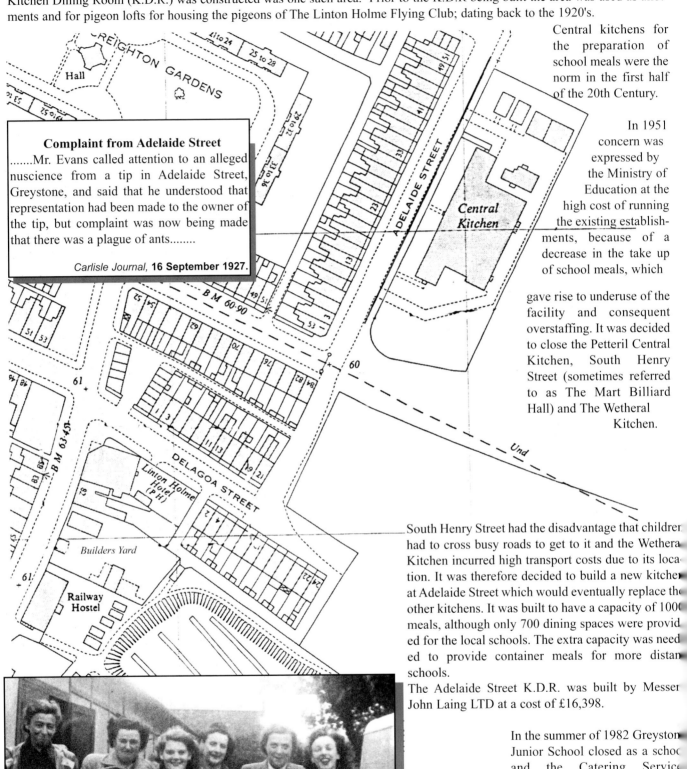

Complaint from Adelaide Street

.......Mr. Evans called attention to an alleged nuscience from a tip in Adelaide Street, Greystone, and said that he understood that representation had been made to the owner of the tip, but complaint was now being made that there was a plague of ants........

Carlisle Journal, **16 September 1927.**

South Henry Street had the disadvantage that children had to cross busy roads to get to it and the Wetheral Kitchen incurred high transport costs due to its location. It was therefore decided to build a new kitchen at Adelaide Street which would eventually replace the other kitchens. It was built to have a capacity of 1000 meals, although only 700 dining spaces were provided for the local schools. The extra capacity was needed to provide container meals for more distant schools.

The Adelaide Street K.D.R. was built by Messer John Laing LTD at a cost of £16,398.

In the summer of 1982 Greyston Junior School closed as a school and the Catering Service changed location to the School premises on Close Street and Edward Street.

The Adelaide Street Kitchen Dining Room facility the became disused. It was later demolished and flats now occupy the area.

Left: The staff from the Wetheral Kitchen Dining Room when it was closing to make way for the Adelaide Street facility in 1950

Harry Turnbull

64

The Metal Box Co. - Botcherby (1955-1999)
Hudson Scott and Sons

10 May 1955. The Town Planning Committee resolved that permission be granted for the development of the area of land compromising 23.9 acres, lying between Borland Avenue and the Railway. The Metal Box Co. LTD. had applied to develop the land as a factory and office building. By **28 October 1955** the sale of land to The Metal Box Co. ltd. was complete.

A Description of the Plant in February 1957
METAL BOX COMPANY FACTORY IN CARLISLE
A factory for the production of 400 million cans a year has been constructed at Botcherby, Carlisle, for the Metal Box Company Limited . The architects are S.N.Cooke and partners. The factory, which has a floor area of 160,000 feet super,comprises a large production area and a loading area with sidings which have been constructed from the main railway into the factory building for direct loading into railway wagons, and there is also a loading area for road haulage. A factory of sixteen 30 ft. bays 240 feet long has been constructed, of which nine bays are production and seven for loading and storing. There is also a large wing for bulk storage of 30 million cans, and there is an office building with a canteen on the first floor. The boiler house contains two oil fired boilers and garages have been constructed adjoining this building. The factory has been designed for six production lines, with overhead conveyors which carry the finished product to the loading areas at a rate of 2,400 cans a minute. In the tinplate area, where 40,000 tons of tinplate per year come into the factory, foundations are supported on 250 piles driven to a depth of 25 feet to take a loading of eight tons per square yard.

It is a steel frame building with brick cladding and north light roof, and preliminary works included raising the site level two feet. Railway works include the construction of an embankment from the main line and sidings, for nearly a mile of track, and there is a turntable for the turn around of wagons inside the factory.

The contract has been carried out with A. Cason as agent and W. Slater is visiting Manager.

Laing's February 1957 Issue of *'The Team Spirit,'*
Carlisle Library

The factory was purpose built for the manufacture of open top cans for the food and beverage market. It was built on a large area to allow room for expansion. The site was originally swamp land, with a rat infested tip on the west side, however, it had to it's advantage a railway running along the back of the site, which was used for the transportation of cans. Local people were trained to run the lines........Botcherby was revolutionary in those days as nobody drank beer from cans.

Recruitment was a problem in the full employment of the early 60s and in

NEW FACTORY.
.......Referring to developments on the open top section of the Company's activities. Sir. Robert (Metal Box Chief) stated: " Work is progressing on the new open top factory at Carlisle, which is to replace the present milk can factory there. With it's equipment, it will cost about £900,000. The initial installation of plant will take place during the summer with a view to obtaining some production in the Autumn......"

Carlisle Journal. **9 June 1956.**

Above: A truck on the turntable at the factory

Above: Early days at Botcherby

A rail truck loaded with cans. Note the loading conveyor at the right of the picture

1960 a Training Centre was set up to organise and run training schemes for school leavers. The Training Centre was extended in 1965 and an extension to the factory was built to house necessary drying ovens and spraying equipment, as the management of the day decided that a move into the manufacture of beer and soft drink cans was the only way forward. Botcherby became the number-one beer can factory.

The Linton Holme Hotel: Building and Opposition

In **July 1887** Saul's solicitors of Carlisle, who incidentally still practice in Castle Street under the name of Saul and Lightfoot, acquired land on Lindisfarne Street from Mr C J Ferguson with a view to building a hotel to serve the newly developing area and to take advantage of the proximity of the North Eastern Railway. By this time the London Road depot was just a goods facility and passengers had to use Citadel Station but, with the increased house building in the area, there were plans to build a new passenger station there. However, this development never came about.

On **29 September 1899** the 'Carlisle Patriot' commented on the proposed hotel: *"....a new road was to be opened to the Railway sheds in the neighbourhood and this house would be planted at the corner leading to and from those sheds."*

Plans for the new hotel were submitted on **17 August 1899**. The architect was A. W. Johnston, also of Castle Street, Carlisle; the founder member of Johnston and Wright of Castle Street today.

The notice of intent to apply for the transfer of the licence from *The Light Horseman'* in Rickergate to the new hotel (see right) was met by strong opposition, not least by the vicar of St. John's; the Reverend C. T. Horan. The final hearing on **29 September 1899** at the Licensing Sessions was a lively one to say the least.

The extract below from the report of the proceedings in the *Carlisle Patriot* illustrates this well. Petitions had been 'got up' by both sides and Mr Errington was acting for the applicants:

"Mr Errington said the applicants had been accused of offering to bribe the magistrates, and of offering a rubbishy public house in exchange for one worth several thousands of pounds more........To say they were offering a bribe by giving up *'The Light horse man'* was to insult the bench and everyone connected with the case.......... His client was a man of position and wealth, and owned thirty of forty acres of building land, which for the next twenty years would be the only available building land in that part of the city. If he went on selling the land as he was doing, some other person might put up a public house, and perhaps that person might not be a responsible or desirable person.

Mr Saul thought that he would take the bull by the horns and erect a public house on his own property, and keep it in his own hands. He had gone to further trouble, since the last court, of testing the opinion of the district. One witness on the last occasion said he objected because he would have difficulty collecting his rents. (Laughter.). He (Mr Errington) now informed the court that eight out of nine of those tenants had signed the petition (now produced) as a protest at the insult thrown at respectable working men.

Mr Westmorland: This is utter rubbish ...etc...........

Mr Errington: You said distinctly you would have trouble collecting your rents. I come prepared (newspaper cuttings) ......

Mr Westmorland: Newspapers are of no account.........

Mr Errington read the extracts, in one of which it was stated that "If there was a public house it would create difficulty collecting his rents" (laughter) and in the other that "he was looking after his own pocket the same as owners of public houses in Rickergate were looking after theirs. (Laughter.) The petition now presented was signed by 430 householders in the district. ....if local option went for anything that should carry it........ only one signature was obtained at each house and 95% were obtained within a radius of a quarter of a mile.... Mr Moscrop, asked as to the distance he went for signatures, said he went the whole length of the street, "the same as the teetotallers did (Laughter.)."

The Rev. T. C. Horan, Vicar of St. John's, presented a list of 62 signatures which he had obtained in Lindisfarne Street against the licence. There are 74 houses in the street. More than half were not teetotallers. -- Mr Errington: Do you consider it fair to canvas your own parishioners? Witness: Quite; I wanted to do it myself. The Rev. A. E. Killon, Congregational Minister, presented a list of 52 signatures against the licence......in Oswald Street. -- Mr Errington said they were chiefly women. -- Witness said he asked for the occupier, in each case, and if he was not in, he asked for the wife. Women had a deep interest in the matter -- Mrs Reed and Mr John Laing, builder, also gave evidence. The latter admitted he was not a teetotaller, but said it was "questionable" if he would grant a licence anywhere. (Laughter.) -- The Bench confirmed the granting of the licence.

To the Governors of the Poor of the Parish of Botchergate, Carlisle: GEORGE MACKAY, Chief Constable of the City of Carlisle: and JOHN BEST of the "Lighthorseman" Inn, Rickergate, Carlisle.

We SILAS GEORGE and GEORGE FREDERICK SAUL of the City of Carlisle, solicitors now residing at Brunstock, near the said City, in the County of Cumberland. **Do Hereby Give Notice** that it is our intention to **Apply** at the **General Licensing Meeting** ......at the Town Hall, Carlisle on the 4th September for a **Provisional Order** authorising the **Removal** of a **Licence** now in force, held by John Best, For the Sale of Intoxicating Liquor to be consumed either on or off the premises......in Rickergate, in this said City and known by the sign of the "Lighthorseman," from which premises I the said Silas George Saul as the owner, from the said premises to a **House** and premises about to be constructed for the purpose of being a **House** for the **Sale** of **Intoxicating Liquors**...... the site of the said proposed house and premises being situate at the corner of Lindisfarne Street and Delagoa Street, in the Parish of Botchergate in the City of Carlisle.

S. G. Saul

G. F. Saul

Carlisle Patriot, **11 August 1899**

Rev. Nigel Davies

The Rev. T. C. Horan, Vicar of St. John's 1899-1904 Formerly a lieutenant in the Royal Indian Marines, he later graduated from Cambridge and was ordained in 1893, before becoming curate of Burneside.

Cumbria Heritage Services, Carlisle Library

The Light Horseman Inn in Rickergate which closed when its licence was transferred to the new Linton Holme Hotel.

Building Workers Conditions in 1899
and What's in a Pub Name ?

The Linton Holme Hotel was built at a cost of about £4000, originally being built to be a residential hotel. It is interesting to consider the conditions under which people worked at this time. A man was expected to work a fifty hour week made up as follows:

5 days of 9 hours from 6a.m. - 4.30p.m.   and 5 hours on a Saturday.

Meal breaks were 8 - 8.30 a.m. and 12 - 1.00p.m.

Tradesman's wage 9d per hour (less than 4p)

Labourer's wage 6d per hour (2 $\frac{1}{2}$p)

Hod Carriers were paid an extra farthing ($\frac{1}{10}$p) per hour because they climbed ladders.

Apprentices began at 4 shillings (20p) per week.

No one was paid for time laid off for bad weather; which was often a problem for those living in our northern climate.

In 1899 mechanical equipment was almost non - existent.

Horses were used as the motive power for almost all road transport and, like a modern vehicle, they had to be well maintained.

If a horse was fed on good hay and oats he could draw a load of 35 cwts (One and three quarter tons) and would probably die at 10 years old.

However, if the horse was not so heavily loaded, fed less oats and put out to grass on summer nights, his life expectancy would increase to around 17 years old.

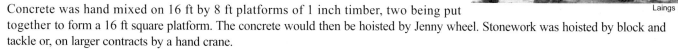

Laings plc.

Concrete was hand mixed on 16 ft by 8 ft platforms of 1 inch timber, two being put together to form a 16 ft square platform. The concrete would then be hoisted by Jenny wheel. Stonework was hoisted by block and tackle or, on larger contracts by a hand crane.

Naming the Hotel, and popular Pub Names and Signs

Pub names often recall long lost traditions. The Pig and Whistle, for example, is derived from the Saxon habit of communally drinking 'e'wassailt. or spiced beer, from a large piggen or pail. The pail was marked inside with ivory pegs to show how much each drinker was allowed. Hence the expression 'taking him down a peg,' when a man's companion drank more than their fair share to deprive him of his 'peg.'

Pub names with religious associations date from the mediaeval boom in pub building, when armies of craftsmen toured Britain building cathedrals and monasteries. They had money to spend and needed places to get their pies and pints.

Many pubs are named after past heroes such as generals and admirals. This is because many soldiers and sailors opened taverns when they retired.

The Linton Holme Hotel takes its name from the area in which it was built, which was then known as Linton Holme. However it was not always described as such in the pre-1930 Carlisle Directories:

Bulmers Directory	1901	Linton Holme Hotel, Lindisfarne Street;	Edmund Blair
Kelly's Directory	1914	Lindisfarne Hotel;	Robert Burden Wray Minns
Carlisle Directory	1921 and 1925	Linden Holme Hotel, Lindisfarne Street;	Robert Milburn

The Pub Sign story began 2000 years ago when the Romans first invaded Britain. The earliest inns, called 'tabernae' or taverns, were built to cater for travellers. A bush of vine leaves was often hung outside to show that wine was for sale, hence the popular name 'The Bush.' Another common name The 'Bag o' Nails' is actually derived from 'Bacchanales,' the festival held in honour of the Roman god of wine. Royalty has played an important role in the development of pubs and pub signs.

Richard III wanted to make it easier for his government officials to check the quality and price of beer sold so, in 1393, he decreed that:- 'whosoever shall brew ale with the intention of selling it must hang out a sign or forfeit his ale.' This had the desired effect and pub signs have proliferated ever since.

William IV is the monarch most depicted on pub signs, in spite of his short reign of only seven years. This is due to the popularity of his 'Beerhouse Act' of 1830; which allowed any householder to open up a beer house upon payment of just two guineas. In a very short time 24,000 new pubs had opened up and many were gratefully named after the King.

Queen Victoria, however, "was not amused" with the "unflattering portraiture" of herself on pub signs and a law was passed which banned any pub sign which depicted the image of a living member of the Royal Family.

With the growth of literacy in the late 19th century brewers began to advertise their beers with large display advertisements on the pub walls and replaced many of the hanging signs with lanterns carrying the brewers name. When the Control Board took over in Carlisle all brewery advertisements were removed; making the pub exteriors very drab and uniform. However, in the 1930s the *Times* newspaper began a campaign to restore pub signs, as they were *the story boards of English history*. Now they are as popular as ever and add their own colour and quaintness to the British pub.

Adapted from a magazine article by *James Dennison*

An Inauspicious Beginning with the first licensee, followed by a more promising future with T. & J. Minns

Edmund Blair was the first licensee of *the Lint* (Linton holme Hotel) and although he did not make a success of his managership, he was obviously well liked in the area. Edmund had previously been the manager of the Samson Inn on London Road and was mentioned fondly by Mildred Edwards in her reminiscences (see page 45). The person stood in the doorway of the Samson (p45) is most likely Edmund Blair, but we cannot be sure. He had one black mark against his name whilst at the Samson as the Licence Records state that on 28 December 1896 he was convicted and fined 40/- (40 shillings or £2) for "permitting drunkenness." However this conviction was later quashed on appeal at the Quarter Sessions. Edmund Blair's tenancy of the Lint was short but not sweet. After only five months of trading he was unable to pay his bills and was made bankrupt.

The *Carlisle Journal,* **7 June 1901** recorded the unhappy event as follows:-

The Linton Holme Hotel in 1902. The Off Sales can be seen to the right. The wall and railings, seen on the pavement, were later removed for the war effort in 1942. The person at the right of the group is Robert Burden Wray Minns, manager of the hotel from 1901 to 1914. Thomas Minns is pictured centre.

"In 1896 Edmund Blair commenced business as a licensed Victualler at the Samson Inn, London Road and carried on the business there until the 2nd February 1901. On the **12 November 1901** he opened the Linton Holme Hotel, Lindisfarne Street and traded there until **17 May 1901** when his goods were sold under distress for rent. On commencing business in 1896 he had no capital of his own, but he borrowed £500 from his brother-in-law ...... his average takings at the Samson Inn being £70 - £75 per week and his average takings at the Linton Holme Hotel £60 - £65 per week. .... on **7 May 1901** a distress was levied at the Linton Holme Hotel for half a years rent, £75, being a quarter rent accrued due and a quarter rent payable in advance, and on the same day the sheriff levied two executions. The whole of the debtors effects were sold for rent.......The debtor has no proposals to make and has been adjudged bankrupt. His liabilities are put at £1436 and his estimated deficiency at £1091......

Carlisle Journal

So ended the first tenancy of the Linton Holme Hotel on a sad note with the landlord made bankrupt and all his worldly goods sold to offset his debt. On **4 June 1901** the licence of the Linton Holme hotel was transferred from Edmund Blair to Messrs. T and J Minns, who were to have a much more successful tenancy.

LINTON HOLME HOTEL, LINDISFARNE STREET, CARLISLE

ROBERT DALTON and SON will Sell by by Auction under Distress for Rent and two writs *a Fi, Fa,* on the premises of the Linton Holme Hotel, Lindisfarne Street, CARLISLE, on WEDNESDAY, May 15th 1901, all the STOCK, FIXTURES, UTENSILS, HOUSEHOLD FURNITURE and EFFECTS of Mr Ed. Blair, Hotel Proprietor, including Drawing Room Suite in Walnut, comprising 4 Conversational Chairs, 2 Easy Chairs and Couch; 1 Bedroom Suite, comprising Dressing Chest with swing mirror : Dressing Table with marble slab and tiled back and 4 Chairs : 2 Chests of Drawers, 3 Full-size Beds and Iron Bedsteads with spring mattresses, 1 Halftester Brass and Iron Bedstead, 4 pairs of Dressing Tables with swing mirrors and marble slabs (nearly new), Kitchen and Bedroom Chairs in variety, Flock and Hailr Mattresses, Feather Beds and a quantity of Bedding, several pairs of Lace Curtains, Walnut Sideboard with Cheffonler base, Walnut Overmantel, Brass Curb Fender with dogs and brasses : Centre, Kitchen and other Tables ; Case Clock, Wringing Machine, a quantity of good Oilcloth, together with an assortment of Pictures, Ornaments, Pots, Pans &c., &c..

At the same time will be sold the BAR FIXTURES and UTENSILS, including Bar Tables, Stools, Pewters, Glasses, &c., &c..

Sale to commence at 1 p.m. to a minute.

Carlisle Journal, **10 May 1901**

The Origins of T & J Minns

Mr Thomas Minns was born in Durham (1843). He was the eldest son of Mr James Minns, one of Durham's first Policemen who wore the memorable tall hat with blue glazed top, blue cut-away-coat and white trousers.

Thomas came to Carlisle as boots to Mrs Rennie of The City Hotel, English Street. Leaving the City Hotel, he entered into the service of a Mr Tarmery at The Bush Hotel, English Street, at the time when through passengers, from Newcastle to the North British Railway, had to be taken by bus from the North Eastern Railway station, London Road, to the Canal station, Port Road. He remained there until the hotel was sold to the Corporation for the purpose of making the Victoria Viaduct. He then entered the service of a Mr James Halstead of Messrs. Halstead and Pearson, wine merchants. Subsequently he held posts with Messrs. Little and Hope, with Mr Joseph Little, and after the retirement of Mr Little, with Mr J.W. Hope. Thomas eventually took over Mr Hope's business, entering into partnership with his son, Mr John Minns, and trading as T. & J. Minns.

Thomas died at his residence in George Street in July 1919, aged 76 years

Cumberland News, **19 July 1914**

Thomas, John and Robert Burden Wray Minns
3 June 1901-1914

Alderman John Minns' life had two phases. The first was when as a Tory politician and as a member of the Licensed trade which clashed with the temperance movement. The second was when his business life led him into catering on non - alcoholic lines and his valuable civic work

As a young man he was assistant to a grocer, Mr Foster, in Denton Holme. Later he became a grocer in his own right It was under his father's auspice that he entered the licensed trade... At one time the Minns' control on the retail side included such prominent licensed houses as *The Wellington* with it's Baronial Hall in English Street and opposite, *The Carlisle Arms*, situated on the island site in front of the Gaol, English Street; and The *Apple Tree,* Lowther Street (also having retail outlets at *The Golden Lion*, Botchergate and The Linton Holme, Lindisfarne Street).

Carlisle Journal, **17 July 1942**

Thomas Minns, hands on hips, in his shop doorway in Denton Holme in the 1890s

It was John Minns' close contact with public houses that gave him a novel idea - a pub without alcohol! The Sarsaparilla Shop was in St. Cuthbert's Lane and sold nothing but soft drinks. T and J Minns also had Minn's Cafe on Botchergate.

Evening News and Star, **26 September 1973**

Robert Burden Wray Minns was the younger brother to Thomas; uncle to John Minns. It was Robert, who was generally listed as the Licensee of the Linton Holme between 1902 and 1914. Robert married Jane Ann Bowerbank in 1899 and they had two children, William James and Francis Isabell. Tragically Jane Ann only survived a few years. In September 1907 she died at the Linton Holme Hotel, leaving her young family motherless. The funeral notice in the *Carlisle Journal* stated that the body was to be interred at Langwathby, leaving the residence at 1.30 p.m. for the Citadel Station (presumably to be carried by train to Langwathby).

It is interesting to relate that a psychic visited the hotel in October 1998. In the ensuing seance she "saw the ghost of the first landlady, who died young and had some connection with a train."

In October 1910, Robert re-married, this time to Mary Ann Bowerbank; second cousin to his first wife. Unfortunately the children did not get on well with their stepmother. She required them to work for her from an early age. Amongst other things, William was made to scrub the floors of the hotel.

On **4 September 1914** Robert Burden Wray Minns died at the hotel from heart failure. His son, William, wasted no time in getting away from his stepmother. He lied about his age in order to join the army and saw service in World War 1. He later joined the Irish Constabulary, then moved to New Guinea and finally to Australia; where he died in 1968. His third wife is still alive and living in Australia.

John Minns outside the *Carlisle City Arms* (Gaol Tap)

Recollections of John Minns, (Grandson of John Minns)

There is a most interesting story regarding a chap 1 used to play with. He was lost during the war in a bombing raid, nobody knew where for 50 years. I found out a Dutchman had done some research on aircraft that had been shot down and had been asking if anyone in Carlisle was still living that knew the airman. This chap lived on Lindisfarne Street. Another playmate was in the Navy on the Royal Oak, blown up at the beginning of the war, he lived in Delagoa Street. My other friend who lived on Sybil Street was in the RAF; he was lost in Holland. Now his father had a few horses and ran a transport business. He had his stables on the spare ground near the river going down Sybil Street. One of his jobs was to collect the props etc. from "The Palace" when it closed on a Saturday night; he would take them to the railway station. Later he ran a small place for making black mortar for building. This was situated in a yard in between the Linton Holme Hotel and the hostel for railwaymen on Lindisfarne Street   (Continued over..........).

Recollections of Mr John Minns
(Grandson of John Minns) (continued)

The River Petteril On Sunday mornings most people would walk their dogs along the bank and stop for a chat. We seemed to have long hot summer holidays and would spend many days going for a *dook* (Swim). Taking with us a home made bottle of Spanish Water made from juice of liquorice from the chemist on Brook Street. We would also fish for sticklebacks and minnows, bringing them home in jam jars. I regret to say that "bird nesting" was carried on, to make a collection. Skylarks were quite common to be heard also kingfishers could be seen among the willows.

Mr John Minns (today)

Games on the Streets.

We played hopscotch; two or three of us skipping, with a long rope. Marbles, were played along the gutters, knocking down cigarette cards; the winner would take the cards. Card Swops; I remember the silk ones from Kensitas with flags of all nations. We played with whip and tops and with hoops, usually made out of steel. Later, the wood cane hoop came out. This followed on to the yo-yo craze in the late 1920s. History, recently, has been repeating itself.
Films at the picture houses were all silent until late 1920. The Palace put on stage shows.

Sweets

We bought our sweets from the corner shops. They included candy eyes, which changed colour as you sucked them, cinder toffee, gob stoppers, liquorice boot laces, sherbet fountains and lucky potatoes; which had a small charm of some kind inside.
All biscuits were sold loose, displayed in tins with glass fronts from a large rack. Other commodities such as pigeon mixture or oats were measured out of open bags stood on the floor.
On Saturday nights the Salvation Army Band used to play outside the *Golden Lion*, then at times outside the *Linton Holme*. Round the streets the ice cream hand cart would come, sometimes a barrel organ .

Characters

The rag and bone man would let you have a goldfish for a bundle of rags, not forgetting the **knife and scissors man** with his sharpening machine (there is one now in Tullie House). At times we would have the **onion man** with his pole on his shoulder swinging strings of onions. The **gypsy women** would call selling clothing pegs which their family would have made. A bit before dusk the **lamp lighter** would be making his rounds, later when clocks were fitted us youngsters would kick the lamp posts to light the lamps. As most of the men were employed on the railway the engine crew were usually woken by a chap called the **bar lad** or **knocker up**. At doors that did not have a doorbell they would rattle the door knocker, you could hear them doors away. It was quite a normal event to see the wives going into the off sales at *The Lint*, with a jug covered with a towel, to fetch a supply of ale for their men folk (see letter of complaint at bottom left of page 79).

Bonfire night

Weeks before November we would go round houses collecting for the bonfire. Any comics would be browsed through then we would store them for the big night. The fire would be 10 to 15 feet high, with old beds, railway sleepers, which would still be burning the next morning. We had plenty of fireworks on the night. The fire was built on the then spare empty ground across from the Linton Holme (now flats). Looking back I am surprised no windows were cracked with the heat of the fire. We did this until around 1940. We would not be able to do this today.

Lindisfarne Street

There were two shops next to the off sales of the Linton Holme, one of them being *Jimmy Carruthers*, shoe and boot repairs.

Oswald Street

There was a general store, *Sowerby's* and also a small baker *Tinns*.

Linton Street

Peter Pierri's fish and chip shop, where we could buy 2p fish and a *penn'orth* of chips.

Corner of Sybil Street (1 Adelaide Street)

This shop (now a house) was empty on and off. It was a paper shop for a good while. Papers such as the *Daily Herald, John Bull and The Sketch*, now long gone, were available. The comics I remember

Public house   Off sales   New shop and house

T and J Minns were not at *The Lint* long before they made additions and alterations. In June 1901 they submitted plans for a shop and house to be built on to the west end of the existing building. The original front elevation plan is shown above

were the: *Boys Own Paper, Rover, Wizard, Adventure, Hotspur, Film Fun, Gem*, and not forgetting *Magnet* with Billy Bunter. The Streets here have an Australian theme, I remember an old map (I have a copy of this). Sydney Street and others were to have been built across from Adelaide Street, which at this time and for many years was a deep rubbish tip. However much later it was filled in and the Kitchen Dining Room (see page 64) was built. This has since been demolished an a small estate built on the site.

Radio or Wireless was here in the early 1920s. one or two houses getting a set. Not many stations were heard, there was usually a tall pole at the bottom of the yard to hold the wire aerial, and if a few people in the room wanted to hear the radio the headphone was placed in a bowl and they would sit round. There was no mains just batteries for the radios, these having to be sent away to be recharged. All houses were lit by **gaslamps.** There would be a piece of really sticky tape hanging from the gaslamp. This was the normal way to catch flies attracted to the light on the dark night.

Health

All streets were surfaced with granite sets. These were wiped over with hot tar, about once a year. Mothers would take their small children to inhale the fumes, as it was thought it would help breathing problems (**scarlet fever** was not uncommon).

Rickets had not yet been completely cured, and many families were large, feeding sometimes up to 7 or 8 or more was a problem. At school a small party of children would walk each day to George Street, where the school clinic was situated, for medication. The **nit nurse** would also visit the school.

Most houses in the district had no bathrooms, and toilets were outside in the yards. In the small courts a single cold water tap was available for the few households. All houses in streets were owned by landlords, rents would be a few shillings, less than 10/- (50p). Wages were around £2 a week old money, a lot less in some cases. Front doors would be left open in summer months. In a lot of cases the key would be hanging on a string behind the letter box, giving you access to it through the flap at any time of the day.

Fusehill (City General) was the workhouse, and all medical matters were dealt with at the **Cumberland Infirmary**. The removal of **tonsils** required you as a child sitting in a row, on a form seat. First one, then another, would be whisked away through the nearest door until all had gone. Once in the recovery room you would lie on a mattress on the floor. After a time you would depart for home, in and out in a few hours. It was usually your first time in a taxi.

The doctor, when visiting your home, would write out the ingredients to make up the contents of your bottle. He would usually be paid on the spot for his attendance.

The chemist (Dalziels, on Brook St.) would roll out the pills and put them in a small round box. The powders would be made up very neatly in so many little paper packets, all made to the same size. We often used to wonder what was in the super sized coloured bottles we saw in his window. Quite a few chemist shops developed films for 6d old money. These would all be done in a tin bath somewhere in the back of the shop and ready for you about 4.30pm., the same day.

Brook Street School

It was a great day when we had *Empire Day* (picture, page 35). This was held in the school yard along with all the flags of the Empire, some children dressing up in costumes and parents attending.

In 1928 **Carlisle Pageant** was held and all schools had a part in it. There was also a yearly event, a large street procession. This we went to see, as it came along Greystone Road onto Warwick Road (I think it started at the Castle went round the streets of Carlisle and back to Bitts Park). It would take about 2 hours to pass. As horse driven transport was the norm, all the horses were dressed up as well as the wagons full of people. It was quite a sight to see.

Pubs

Darts, cards, or any sort of gambling were not allowed in the pubs until the late 1940s. Usually we enjoyed a chat, a drink and dominoes. There was always a good fire.

John Minns.

By **1910** T. and J. Minns had interests all over the city. The letter heading below provides a good indication of the extent of their wine and spirit business at that time.

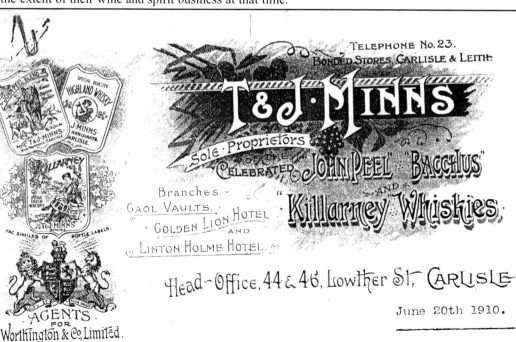

An example of a non alcoholic beverage produced by T and H Minns

Nick Horton

A Nostalgic Journey to the Pubs of Old Carlisle

In 1973 the *Evening News and Star* published a story, thought to have been written by John Minns, which mentions many of the pubs in Carlisle at the time, before State Control. Can you spot them all?

Passing through the Citadel accompanied by the City Commercial, we met Wellington, who had just returned from a voyage round the Globe. He had sailed in a ship called Albion, which was under the command of Nelson, he being most able to attend to the Old Anchor. During his travels, he purchased a White Horse, a Bay Horse and a Golden Lion, also a Red and a Green Dragon, which he intended to present to the Oddfellows. On second thoughts he had them taken to the Hole in the Wall in charge of the Guardsman and the Jovial Sailor, to be conveyed by the Wagon and Horses, having lost Three Horseshoes, to the Prince of Wales, who had arrived by the Caledonian Railway and had taken up his quarters in the County.

On arrival there we found that William James had placed the Wool Pack and the Golden Fleece, along with the Hare and Hounds, in the Baronial Hall, but with the aid of Samson and Goliath we succeeded in making an entrance to the Crown and Mitre, where we saw a terrible fight between George and the Dragon. We were startled by the tolling of the Blue Bell, followed by a report from the Three Cannons. On turning round, by the light of the Rising Sun, we saw the Coach and Horses coming along, bearing the Lorne Arms and driven by Shakespeare. It had the Friars on top, who were whispering something into the Old Queen's Head about the Old Black Bull having met with a terrible death through trying to swallow a Pineapple. All this time, the Jovial Hatter and the Jolly Butcher were hard at work, pushing the Plough past the Old Bush on to the Turf, when up came the Sportsman, who told us he had seen the Light Horseman chasing the White Ox under the Royal Oak, which so enraged the Queen, who with the Horse and Farrier was just coming over the Petteril Bridge, that she picked up the Quarter of Mutton and threw it at the Duke's Head, who retaliated by picking up the Crown and Anchor. He hurled them at the Saracen, missed him and hit the Lion and Lamb, who were reclining under the Barley Stack, frightened the Fox and Hounds, upset the Wheatsheaf and knocked the Old Black Bull under the Apple Tree, maiming the Green Man. He was lifted up in the Maltster's and the Coachmakers Arms and conveyed to the Great Central, where he was carefully attended by the Angel. As a reward she received the Three Crowns, which suggested refreshment, so accompanied by the Pedestrian and with the assistance of the Masons, Bricklayers and Spinners, they adjourned to the Bowling Green and witnessed a fight between the Dog and Bull. After ordering the Fish, which was in the Anglers Arms, to be given to the Otter, they formed themselves into a Union. With the Spread Eagle as a motto, they decided that a Bird in Hand was worth Two in the Bush.

Mr John Minns, author of the above ditty, He is pictured here with John Peel's Horn and Whip.

A 1910 Bank holiday outing by charabanc. Photo provided by Mary Gibson, aged 80, of Brook Street. Mary was born at No. 2 Sybil Street (now Johnston's Hairdresser). Her father is seated on the second row from the front, third face along, immediately above the man standing in front of the bus.

Robert Milburn, Licensee (1916 - 1924)

On the **4 September 1914** Robert Burden Wray Minns, licensee of the 'Lint' died at the hotel, aged 67 years, yet no change of licensee appeared in the Carlisle Directory until 1920. However the records of the Central Control Board show that when they acquired the Linton Holme Hotel in 1916, the licensees were Robert Milburn. Margaret Slee lived in the adjoining house in Lindisfarne Street, to the right of the shop. They would probably have taken over in 1914 after the death of Mr Minns. At this time a pub manager's wage was about £1-15s (£1- 75p).

Robert Burden Wray Minns' grave
in Carlisle Cemetery

The Origins of the Liquor Control Board

During the building of the railways in the 1840s, as with the building of the Canal in the 1820s, there was a large influx of itinerant labour to the city. These navvies, essential to get the job done, were a wild lot and problems with drunkenness and riotous behaviour caused difficulties for the authorities and townspeople alike. During World War 1 the problem arose again. Thousands of workers were drafted in to build and work for the massive munitions depot at Gretna. Previously only earning a few shillings per week, they now earned about £20. They had money to burn, and drink was cheap. A bottle of spirits was under 10s. (50p) and a beer only 2d. or 3d. (1p) a pint. They sent money home to their families, paid for their lodgings and food and still had money left to buy more alcohol than a man could drink.

The growth of drunkenness was gradual at first but by spring 1916 disorder had spread to such an extent "as to threaten and undermine the ordinary social life of the city." An eye witness at the time related: "Some 5000 of the said navvies nightly remove themselves from the scene of their labour to Carlisle, with the result that a once respectable city, chiefly notable for it's Castle, it's Cattle Market and it's hanging of rebels, has become a city of dreadful Saturday nights."

The Chief Magistrate said publically: "Unless something is done the place will soon become completely demoralised...."

Lloyd George fearing that riots would take place, as was happening in Ireland at the time (many of the navvies being Irish), introduced the Liquor Control Board. This scheme was thought to be only a temporary measure but it became known as the *Carlisle Experiment* and was to last 55 years, during which time it was to be praised and hated.

Adapted extract from *A City Under The Influence.* by John Hunt.

June 1916
The Control Board decided to conduct the retail licensed trade of the district and that of salaried management. The Board believed in this way it could maintain a closer supervision of the sale of intoxicants. The Board then spent the next 3-4 months acquiring the 119 licensed premises and 7 registered clubs in Carlisle. once acquired many premises were closed and the four breweries serving Carlisle were centralised into one.

Managers were appointed by the Board and were paid a regular wage of £8 - £10, less than if they were left free to manage the old way. These appointed managers had to have no interest of any kind in the sale of alcoholic liquors. This resulted in an almost immediate effect of reducing drunkenness.

December 1916
The Board had introduced restrictive measures which applied to all licensees:

The only days and hours which intoxicants can be sold or supplied are as follows

On Sales.	ALE, BEER & WINE.	Weekdays 12 noon to 2.30 p.m.	and	6 p.m. to 9 p.m.
Off Sales.	ALE. BEER & WINE	Weekdays 12 noon to 2.30 p.m.	and	6 p.m. to 8 p.m.
	SPIRITS	The same (except on Saturday, when no Spirits can be sold or supplied).		
Sundays	No intoxicants may be sold or supplied either for 'on' or 'off' consumption.			
Rationing	A set amount of intoxicants was allotted to each house, divided into specific portions per opening period.			

Managers were instructed to stop serving after they had taken, in any opening period, a preset amount of money.
The quantity allowed to each customer was strictly allotted as follows:
Midday Opening - Beer served in 1/2 pints only.
Spirits served in half glasses.
The sale of drink during summer months was not permitted until 7 p.m.

Advertisement

The advertisement of intoxicants was forbidden. There was little to suggest that a building was a public house except for names or signs.

The number of Off sales outlets were reduced from over 100 to between 15 and 18 and grocers licenses were abolished.

At the request of the factory there was a local suspension of 'on' sales of spirits in the neighbourhood of the Gretna Munitions Factory.

The sale of intoxicating liquor was limited to 'over 18's, except for consumption with meals.

Treating

It became illegal to buy drinks for friends: "Everybody must order and pay for his own drinks. You must not therefore. serve anybody with intoxicants unless they are ordered and paid for by the person himself, nor must anyone drink intoxicants for which he has not paid."

Note the use of "his" and "he" in this instruction to the licensee. At this time public houses were for men. The women were expected to remain at home caring for the man's family.

The reason for the "No Treating" rule was that the landlord had to ration the drink per man to 1 pint at each opening session. Heavy drinkers would try to get round this by ordering a 'round' at the bar for their mates and then would retire to a quiet corner to drink it all themselves.

Tullie House Museum & Art Gallery

Hotels and Food Taverns.

If your house is a hotel or food tavern the following special rules apply:

A visitor actually living in the licensed premises may drink intoxicants during prohibited hours, provided they are supplied and paid for during the times mentioned.

Intoxicants ordered and drunk with a meal may be paid for when the meal is paid for, but before the person who has drunk the liquor has quitted your premises.

A person who is paying for a meal for somebody else can pay for intoxicants consumed by the other person at the meal, as well as his own food.

Extracted and adapted from *A city under the influence*, John Hunt.
and *Central Control Board Records,* Carlisle Castle Archives.

In **1919** the Board began to relax on some of the restrictions it had imposed as war measures. This led to the Liquor Control Board getting a lot of '*bad press.*' **Sunday opening** was to be resumed. This, predictably, created a lot of opposition from The Womens' League and the Tee Totallers of the City, who feared a return to the public disorder which had occurred previously.

SUNDAY OPENING IN CARLISLE
List of Houses to be available.

At a special meeting held on Tuesday the local Advisory of the Central Control Board (Liquor Traffic) decided that the following houses, about two thirds the total, should remain open on Sundays.
...................Jovial Sailor Inn, Caldcotes; Linton Holme Hotel, Lindisfarne Street; London Road Tavern. London Road;............................

Carlisle Journal, 7 February 1919

On **10 February 1919** the *Cumberland News* reported that
Bar Maids were declining to come to work in protest at the resumption of Sunday opening .

At this time the wages for a bar maid ranged from 21 shillings 9 pence, if in service less than three months, to 25 shillings 3 pence, if in service for more than three months.

Over the next few months the rules continued to be relaxed. Drinking hours were extended, first of all to 9.30 p.m., in March 1919, and then to 10 p.m. in May 1919. There were complaints in the press that beer and spirits were more expensive in Carlisle than elsewhere, due to an additional 25 shilling charge per barrel, levied by the Food Controller, and that alcoholic drinks were "weaker" and "more scarce" than else-where in the country. In 1915 Mr Lloyd had stated that "the Liquor Board should only be given powers for a period not exceeding 12 months after Peace was declared" and in 1919 there were demands for it to go.

12 December 1919

It was reported that ......" the Carlisle Experiment of the Liquor Control board had been a success in reducing drunkenness in the city......" The figures on the left were given.

Drunk with two Control Board glasses in his pocket

A sketch from the Rev. W. Stuart's booklet on The Carlisle and Annan Experiment in State Purchase and Liquor Nationalisation. 1916-17.

Cumbria Heritage Services, Carlisle Library

Further sketches appear on the next page.

Public Order in Carlisle Total Convictions for Drunkenness		
1914		275
1915	1st nine months 107	
	last 3 months 170	277
1916	1st nine months 564	
	last 3 months 389	953
1918		80

The replacement of the Control Board by the 'State Management Scheme'

The Licensed Victuallers Gazette waded into the fray with the following comments:

1. Carlisle should never have been penalised for drunkenness caused by the introduction of thousands of workmen into the district to do war work "Drunkenness amongst munition workers is doing more damage in the war than all the German submarines put together." *Lloyd George.*

2. There had been such a reduction in the number of licensed houses to an extent that public requirements cannot be met on Saturday nights.

3. The old social life of the inn and friendly relations which existed between landlords and their customers had been destroyed.

4. The Control Board had spent lavishly and only managed to keep costs down by centralising four breweries into one.

However it was not until the introduction of the **Licensing Act of 1921** that the Control Board was abolished and The Carlisle and District State Management Scheme evolved. Some of the heavy handed rules were relaxed, however it was still thought to be a temporary measure.

The Carlisle undertaking was by way of an 'Experiment.' It was an experiment that appeared to be going wrong, as the first year under the State Management Scheme saw an increase in the number of convictions for drunkenness:

"There is much boozing and drunkenness in Carlisle under State purchase and State Management. Considering the number of Houses has been reduced, unemployment and high beer and spirit prices are making excessive drinking much harder. The number of convictions in 1921 are nearly twice as great as in 1918. These drunken cases were of men and women.

Carlisle was compared to Newcastle:

"Carlisle under Government Management has had an increase in convictions. Newcastle was still under the old Private Management has had a decrease in convictions for drunkenness...."

An eye witness said :

"*It is fair to say that Carlisle, at least on Saturday and Sunday nights is a boozing drunken City.*"

Mr. Spence (Chief Constable) in reply : "*I do not consider that drunkenness on this scale in a city of the size of Carlisle presents any serious problems.*"

National Press.

---

23 Old Greystone,
CARLISLE
7th January, 1919

Dear Sir,

Yesterday evening I did not feel disposed to leave my house so at my request my wife went to one of the houses under your control and asked for 3 gills of beer. The person in charge declined to serve her saying that they were short, upon which she was asked if she would supply a pint seeing that they were short, she said no "<u>you are not a customer.</u>" Will you kindly inform me if your instructions to the managers refer in any way to customers or non-customers.

Or, on the other hand, is the "Public" placed in the absurd position, that the more temperate members of it are liable to be penalised with impunity, at the whim of a paid servant of the "State".
Any information on the above, will oblige,

Yours,

(Sgd) John M. Hilton

To.

Sir Edgar Sanders.

Above: A letter of complaint regarding refusal of service at the Lint

---

Some Inn Keepers had begun to refuse to supply meals and serve drinks, such as tea, because they did not think the profit repaid them for the trouble involved. As a result managers were reminded that they must serve food when it was asked for and they must serve it in a cleanly way and at a fair price.

1927. Criticism of the State Management Scheme came from the clergy as well: "During the war I saw soldiers become the victims of fast girls and free women frequenting Board Houses, drinking, soliciting, and going off with them. I submit the considered opinion and evidence that the Womens' Bars provided by the management simply had the effect, and were for the purpose, of segregating many of the lowest, most vicious unattended women, who, many of them go there *for a certain purpose;* the residue being those who do not object to associate with them. These *womens' bars* are small cubicles which I almost invariably found overcrowded, and with the air very bad on Saturday nights .

There were no *womens' bars* in Carlisle public houses before the advent of State Management. I have more than once witnessed

Good old sport ! !

Cumbria Heritage Services, Carlisle Library

a rather tightly jammed crowd of women dancing up and down in gross alcoholic abandon. On Saturday night at closing time fifty percent of the men issuing from a house in a rough locality were drunk, and seventy five percent of the women from the *womens' bars*... I have put my head into some of these bars to be told; "The next compartment, love," or to be greeted with obscene, language or immodest suggestion. I have been accosted by young women coming out of these bars... .I have witnessed the most shocking drunkenness and have been treated to the most vile invitations by women in these bars."

Drink Nationalisation in England and It's Results, Rev. Wilson Stuart **1927.**

Two women and a man holding each other up

Cumbria Heritage Services, Carlisle Library

Richard Wright, Licensee (1924-24 April 1940)

All the protests against the Carlisle and District State Management Scheme were to no avail and it would continue to control the Licensed Premises and Managers for many years to come; until the 1970s.

The Directory Records for 1924 show that Mr. Richard Wright was now Licensee of the Linton Holme Hotel. An exact date is hard to pinpoint due to the lack of early records available.

The following bar price list dates from the early 1920s and one just like it probably hung in the Linton Holme Hotel

Public Bar Price List

Draught

Ale	6d. per pint	3d. per ½ pint
Bitter Beer	8d. per pint	4d. per ½ pint
Stout	8d. per pint	4d. per ½ pint

Bottled Beer and Stout.

Local...	6½d. per ½ pint bottle
Guiness.......................................	7½d. per ½ pint bottle
Bass..	7½d. per ½ pint bottle
Worthingtons..............................	7½d. per ½ pint bottle
Cider............................ 5d. small bottle	8d. large bottle

Whisky

Border Blend
Johnnie Walker   6½d.   Per small glass
Jameson
Dewar White Label   1s / 1d.   Per large glass
Black and White
White Horse

Minerals etc.

Beer and Stout Substitutes	4d.	per bottle
Soda Water (Local)	3½d.	per bottle
Soda Water (Schweppes)	5d.	per bottle
Ginger Ale (Local)	4d.	per bottle
Ginger Ale (Ross, Schweppes etc.)	6d.	per bottle

Below: The food provided in pubs in the 1930's was not as varied or as international as the range of pub food currently found in many pubs in the 1990's, but it was good wholesome British food as this menu from that time illustrates.

Menu

Lentil Soup	2d
Cod Steak and Chips........................	6d
Roast beef and Vegetables..............	11d
Steak and Kidney Pudding and Veg..	1/-
Liver and Potatoes............................	6d
Rissoles..	3d
Hot Beef Pies...................................	3d
Hot Pot...	2d
Potatoes..	2d
Butter Beans....................................	1d
Beetroot...	1d
Steamed Ginger Pudding and Custard.	3d
Rice Pudding....................................	2d
Sandwiches various	1½ to 2d
Tea...	2d
Coffee...	3d
Oxo...	3d

Below: A charabanc is about to leave from the 'Lint' circa 1930 on a day trip. According to Ronnie Chandler (see page 62), the large man in the middle of the photograph was a slaughterman, Bob Cockburn.

The man at the rear window is that of Mr Henry (Harry) Chandeler, the window cleaner at the time and the grandfather of Ronnie.

Recollections from the early days at the 'Lint'

In the early days at the Linton Holme Hotel refreshments were often dispensed in brass jugs like those in the photograph. Brass gallon, half gallon, quarts, and pint measures, right down to spirit measures were used. The Railwaymen would come into the hotel at about 7 a.m. each morning and would be served rum and hot milk out of these pots.

During the 1920s and 1930s the public continued to complain about the overcrowding and reduced hours of opening in Carlisle compared with other parts of the country.
A critic in the *Daily News* remarked:
Few pubs and few hours involve overcrowded bars, quick standing drinking, excitement and increased drunkenness. The rational social enjoyment of a pipe and a glass is made impossible.

A report in the national press in 1922 stated:
womens bars were becoming crowded too, and an increase of 'secret' drinking amongst women was giving cause for concern, so steps were being taken to have all back doors of licensed houses closed for the sale of intoxicants, believing that such an action would reduce the 'temptation' to many women."

John Dixon (photo, page 6) recalls that in those days the Linton Holme was made up of many separate rooms. **Smoke Room 1** (see the map below) became the **Refreshment Room** (todays 'Bikers'' Corner') and **Smoke Room 2** (now the darts alley) were for both sexes. The **Bar Parlour**, which had a serving hatch through to the **Snug**, was for men only. John recalls that men who thought themselves of a higher class than the rest of us would sit in the **Bar parlour** (sometimes christened the 'Snob'), they were usually the older regulars. Today the room is situated to the right of the entrance and is used by the 'Domino School,' which consists mainly of old timers, such as John and his friends. In those days each room had a bell for room service. Beer cost 4d. a pint and a penny extra for room service.

There was much resentment amongst the local people at the restrictions which applied in Carlisle due to the State Management Scheme, compared with other parts of the country. This occasionally led to letters in the paper as illustrated below.

Carlisle and Its Public Houses
We working chaps who use them never seem to have our opinion asked as to how we like them. It always seems to me as if all our laws and regulations as to what we shall eat and drink, what time we shall get up in the morning and what time we shall go to bed at night have to be made by those busybodies who call themselves guardians. Those who have comfortable houses and good cellars go to them anytime they like.
I think it is about time we who pay three times as much for a pint of ale and four times for a glass of whiskey should take a hand in the game. We have votes and shall use them. It's time things were put back in their old place. Yours Truly,
A Working Man
Cumberland News, 1922

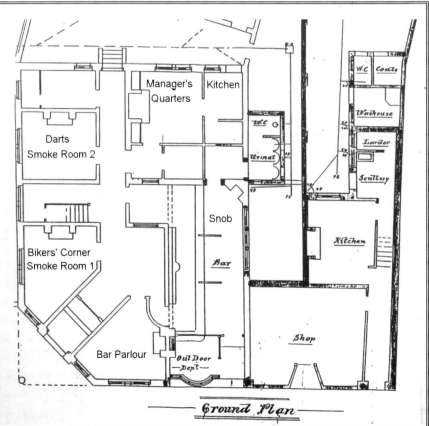

The original plan of the Lint in 1900 when the shop was added. The 'arial' font text (e.g. Bikers'' Corner) has been added to the original plan, to relate to the pub today. The doors to the partitioned rooms have been removed, as have some of the partitions.

81

Pigeon Racing
The Linton Holme Flying Club

The Linton Holme Flying Club met regularly in the Linton Holme Hotel, sometimes with their pigeons. Mrs Eva Douglas (see page 88), a former cleaner at the Lint, recalls that members would meet on a Friday to set the pigeon timers. On Sunday the pigeons were displayed in boxes round the pub and on Monday she had a lot of feathers to clean up. Pigeon racing has long

been a popular pastime of the northern working man. Pigeons have served man in several ways over the years. Originally bred as a food source, the homing instinct of pigeons was soon recognised and put to good use as a rapid means of communication. Solomon is alleged to have transmitted orders through his entire kingdom by means of homing pigeons and, in the early years of the last century, the news of victory at Waterloo was brought to this country by homing pigeon. Pigeons were extensively used in the Franco-Prussian War of 1870 and also in the South African War of 1899 -1902. Pigeons became indispensable when the movement of men was considered too dangerous. In the two world wars many thousands of lives were saved by the use of carrier pigeons to communicate information.

The winner of the East Cumberland Federation old bird race from Nantes (530 miles) by one hour, owned by the Petteril View Loft.
Carlisle Journal, 8 August 1930

The sport of Long Distance Pigeon Racing developed at the same time as the railway system. The Linton Holme was heavily populated by railway workers. The sport did not become organised on a national basis until 1897, when the Royal Pigeon Racing Association was formed. Unfortunately there appear to be no surviving records of the pigeon club at the Linton Holme, so we must rely on the recollections of older inhabitants and articles from the sports pages of the *Carlisle Journal.*

A racing pigeon can cost anything from £20 to the highest price paid so far of £106,000. Each pigeon carries a secretly numbered rubber band in addition to its permanent identity ring. On arrival home the rubber ring is removed and placed in a tamper proof clock, which stamps the exact time of return. The distance from the release point to each loft is known to the nearest yard. Pigeon races are decided by 'velocity proper,' that is to say, the pigeon flying the greatest number of yards per minute wins the race. To obtain this the time taken to fly the race is divided into the distance between the release point and the loft.

On **15 July 1938** the *Carlisle Journal* carried an article about Mr Jerry Turnbull, pigeon fancier.

"...he is one of the younger school, and (although he now has a number of good performances to his credit) a more ardent and devoted fancier it would be hard to find. He has been flying pigeons for about 10 years, starting when he was 13, and joining the Edenvale Club in 1928. During his first year he flew in partnership with a brother to a loft at the rear of his home in Brook Street. About a year later he moved to the loft's present site at Linton Holme. Although he is now on his own he has the interest and assistance of his uncle, Mr Harry Turnbull and a friend, Mr Fred Baxter............ As well as flying in the Edenvale Club."

"LOFTY" WORK. -- Clocking in a bird after the Carlisle Flying Club's race from Bath.   *Carlisle Journal,* 17 October 1930

Jerry Turnbull, 15 July 1938

Pigeon Racing

The loft at Linton Holme is a neat affair, over 50 feet long and about 6 feet wide, housing 32 old birds and about 30 youngsters. The narrowness of the loft was the first feature I noticed, and the fact that when you are inside you rub shoulders with the birds, so to speak, may be one of the reasons why the birds are so quiet.

Carlisle Journal , 26 May 1939

Bank Holiday Trips and the sudden death of a Manager

Every Bank Holiday for years on end the regulars at the Lint went on a bus trip. They always took plenty of drink and sandwiches with them and, irrespective of any other arrangements, it was an unwritten rule that they always got back in time for last orders at the 'Lint.'

A Bank Holiday Outing from the Lint in the 1930s

Several people in the photograph above have been identified as listed below: NK = Not Known

SMT bus driver	Gill (hairdresser) 'Le Gall' Devonshire St.	Alf Surtees	Bob Cockburn (Slaughter House)	McConnell Footballer Carlisle Utd.	Grundy	NK	Douglas	Eden	NK	Scott	NK	NK	NK	NK
NK	NK	Swan	NK	Albert Laing	Dan Johnston in shop in Blackfriars St.	NK	NK	NK	Jose Laing Stone Mason	NK	NK			

Richard Wright's career as licensee of the Linton Holme Hotel came to a sudden and tragic end on **28 April 1940**.

Mr Wright was found seriously ill in his bedroom on the Saturday evening by his housekeeper. He was removed to the Cumberland Infirmary and then transferred to the City General Hospital, where he died. Extracts from the transcript of the inquest into his death, as published in the Carlisle Journal, are reproduced on the right.

Carlisle Hotel Manager Found In Gas - Filled Room: Inquest Story

The inquest on Mr Richard Wright, manager of The Linton Holme Hotel, who died after being found seriously ill in his room on April 28th. was resumed before the Deputy City Coroner at the City Police Office on Friday. Isabelle Jennings, who was housekeeper to the deceased, stated that Wright had gone upstairs to rest at about 3.45 p.m. on Saturday afternoon and as he had not come downstairs at six, she opened the door of his bedroom and found him sitting in a chair underneath a gas bracket on the wall. The room appeared to be full of gas and she could hear it escaping from the gas bracket. Wright appeared to be unconscious so, after opening the windows she laid him on the floor and loosened the clothing round his neck. .... Percy Adams Bailey, 29 Sebergham Terrace, who was called to the house by the last witness, stated he felt Wright's pulse and got a faint response. He advised Mrs Jennings to send for a doctor and continued the artificial respiration until he arrived. Constable Hale said that in reply to a telephone message he took an ambulance to the Linton Holme Hotel.............. Details of a post mortem examination of the body were given by Dr Faulds, Pathologist at the Cumberland Infirmary. In his opinion death was due to carbon monoxide poisoning. Bringing in his verdict the coroner stated that the deceased had left a letter which made it quite clear that he took his own life while the balance of his mind was temporarily disturbed. *Carlisle Journal,* 21 May 1940

Austin Little, licensee 1940 - 1952

After the death of Richard Wright, Mr F Elliot was appointed as relief manager. State Management Records still exist from this time and so much more is known about the day to day running of the Lint from 1940 onwards than previously. There were many applications for the position of manager of the Linton Holme, from managers already employed in public houses around Carlisle and District. One such application was that of Austin Little, who was manager of the Bridge End at Dalston.

Austin had a wooden leg and this was commented on by the State Management Board, when considering his application, as follows:

Little has lost a leg, but this disability does not unduly interfere with his managership duties."

Austin was successful in his application and took up his post on **5 August 1940.** It is interesting to note the terms and conditions of a tenancy at this time when working for the State Management Scheme (see right).

Austin Little asked permission from his employers for his sister in law and child to live at the hotel, whilst his brother was in the army. This was agreed and she would take on barmaid duties in return. However it was soon discovered that her husband, Little's brother was stationed in Carlisle and was also living at the hotel. The family was duly charged six shillings a week as a contribution towards heating and lighting costs.

At this time there were two sisters, known as the sisters McPherson, who were employed as char-women. They worked two and a half hours every day, seventeen and a half hours a week and were paid accordingly. During the winter months they would work four extra hours as there were four fire places to be cleaned. Later, due to the extra trade on a weekend it was decided that they could work an extra hour on Sundays and Mondays.

Apparently they had suffered many delays due to lack of hot water and so they took it upon themselves to take it in turns to start fifteen minutes earlier to light the boiler fire, thus ensuring that hot water was available when needed. Austin Little's employers, on

This Agreement made the **fifth** day of **August** one thousand nine hundred and **forty** ---- BETWEEN his Majesty's Principal Secretary of State for Home Affairs (hereinafter called 'the employer') by Albert Ernest Mitchell the General Manager of the Carlisle and District State Management Scheme being duly authorised in his behalf by the Employer of the one part and **Austin Little**

(hereinafter called 'the manager') of the other part. **WHEREAS** by virtue of the Licensing Act, 1921, the premises known as the **Linton Holme Hotel** situate at **Lindisfarne Street., Carlisle** in the County of Cumberland together with the goodwill, furniture and effects thereof are vested in the Employer and the business therof is conducted as part of the Carlisle and District State Management Scheme.......... The Manager shall be allowed to occupy the said premises free of rent, rates and taxes, and shall be provided free of cost with a reasonable and sufficient supply of fuel and light........ The Manager shall personally reside at the said premises during the continuation of this agreement and shall not, without consent of the Employer, sleep away from the premises, nor be absent from the premises during the hours when intoxicating liquor may be lawfully sold............ The Manager shall at all times when the house is open be ready to supply to the public, on demand, food of a reasonable kind and quantity and non-intoxicating drinks such as meat extracts, tea, coffee and cocoa..........

The Employer shall pay to the Manager for his services, including assistance rendered to him by his wife, a salary of **Four pounds two shillings and six pence** per week..........

AS WITNESS the hands of the parties hereto the day and year first before written.

Signed by the said Austin Little

in the presence of:-

Receipt No. **10/ 73017**

MINISTRY OF WORKS AND BUILDINGS.

SALVAGE OF RAILINGS, ETC.

———————

In Exercise of the Powers conferred under Sections 50 and 53 of the Defence (General) Regulations, 1939, the Railings of this Property have been removed.

To Owner or Occupier, *Linton Holme Hotel*

Address *Delagoa St Carlisle*

Contractor's Name *Demolition & Construction Co*

Address *34 Moorfields Liverpool 2*

Foreman's Signature *John Potts*

Date *23/5/42*

---

hearing of this, suggested that he should make it part of his duties to have the fire lit in time.

On **12 April 1942** Mr J W Allison was appointed holiday relief manager until 26 April 1942. Mr Allison would himself become a permanent manager of the 'Lint' at a later date.

In order to help the war effort owners of premises throughout the Britain were encouraged to remove the iron railings from their buildings. This was to have a drastic effect on the appearance of buildings in Carlisle, which is still with us today. On **23 May 1942** a works order was made out to remove the railings from the Linton Holme Hotel (see left). Owners could claim twenty five shillings (£1.25) a ton compensation for railings removed.

In **March 1949** Austin Little applied for one months summer holiday so that he could go on a motor tour with friends in Normandy. He offered to give up his two weeks winter leave to allow for this.

His request was refused and correspondence from C R Pension Esq.,

The Post War Years and the Return of Darts to City Pubs

Superintendent for the Carlisle and District State Management Scheme, to the General Manager read:

.........I am not surprised at the request as, of course there is no end to what employees now expect, but I do foresee considerable trouble and further applications of a similar type if this door is ever opened.

Perhaps not surprisingly the request was refused. The reference to the 'expectations of employees' obviously came from the fact that, after a strike threat in 1948, long negotiations between the managers and employers resulted in a substantial improvement in pay, holiday entitlement and sick pay conditions for state management employees. Under this new agreement Austin Little received £6-10s -0d (£6.50) per week and his wife was paid thirty shillings (£1.50) for assisting. His holiday entitlement was increased to two weeks in the summer and two weeks in the winter, this at a time when most working men only received one or two weeks holiday a year. Smokers might be interested in the low cost of cigarettes and tobacco at this time (see right).

5 March 1949 saw the return of dart playing to city pubs. The *Cumberland News* reported:

"Some months ago there was sharp criticism of the Carlisle and District State Management Scheme for not providing darts in the State controlled taverns. The explanation given officially was that dart throwing in public was dangerous and that few, if any, of the houses were of suitable construction for playing the game. About 40 inns in the City and surrounding district have been selected for the initial 'try out,' the safety of the public and the seating and the furnishings of the houses being the main considerations......About 36 dart boards have so far been installed......."

In **1950** however a weekend ban was imposed. The Cumberland News reported on the *outburst of indignation in the majority of State Management public houses in the City and surrounding district by the latest order of State Management Authorities that the playing of darts will not be permitted at the weekends.* The manager of one of the taverns where the game has been very popular since it was introduced stated that the authorities had made a great mistake. *As far as I am aware there have been no complaints and there have certainly been no accidents. It is useless permitting darts on the first four days of the week only, when the taverns are comparatively empty. Money is much shorter now and it is only at the weekends that the working men can afford to come into the house for a pint and a game of darts. Dart playing is as much a recreation as dominoes, billiards, snooker and table bowls, which are still permitted on Fridays and Saturdays.*

Another manager stated the darts players resented this interference with their liberties from London. *These people know nothing of the conditions in Carlisle and District and couldn't care less..... The managers should be allowed to use their discretion in this matter. I detest this remote control.*

Cumberland News

In spite of the protests the ban was not lifted until **May 1952** and then only partially (see right).

The State Management Records at this time also show that in **May 1952** Managers were allowed to have T.V. sets in their living quarters. This was in spite of the worry, prevalent at the time, of the possibility of an aerial being struck by lightning and causing a fire.

In 1943 the hotel had been in much more danger from fire. There had been problems with electrical fuses blowing for no apparent reason. An inspection by David Thompson and sons recommended the re-wiring of the hotel in the interests of public safety. Nothing was done immediately but, after several more incidents of fuses blowing, it was decided to have the hotel re-wired at a cost of £72.

Unfortunately for Austin Little he was not able to enjoy the experience of having the new fangled television in his home.

On **14 July 1952** he died tragically of a coronary thrombosis at the hotel. Austin was only 52 years old.

Joseph William Allison, known as *'Big Bill'* to his customers, who had previously acted as relief manager for the Linton Holme hotel, took over as Licensee in September 1952.

1948 Prices
Cigarettes & Tobacco

Woodbines	10	for	1s 3½d	(7p)
	20	for	2s 7d	
Gold Flake				
Capstan	10	for	1s 9d	(9p)
Players Navy Cut	20	for	3s 6d	
Craven 'A' etc.				
Twist Tobacco		3s 6½d	per ounce	

BAN LIFTED FROM DARTS IN STATE TAVERNS

PROTEST SUCCEEDS

The ban on week-end dart playing in the State taverns at Carlisle has been lifted.

The ban was imposed because, in the crowded conditions of the inns on Friday and Saturday nights, dart throwing was considered to be dangerous.

Dart players protested that these were the most popular nights for the game, because working men were in possession of their pay packets.

Mr. J. Henderson, general manager of the State Management Scheme, called into consultation the Tavern Managers. As a result of negotiations it has been decided that in the city taverns dart playing will be allowed on Friday evenings until closing time (ten o'clock) and on Saturday evenings up to seven o'clock. In the county inns within the State control area play is to be allowed at the discretion of the managers.

No Sunday games of any kind are permitted in the State taverns.

Joseph William Allison, Licensee (1952 -1971)

Joseph William Allison ('Big Bill') was transferred from The Board Inn (today The Boardroom) in Castle Street. He began his duties at 11 a.m. His wage was £7 - 2s per week and that of his wife £1 - 10s per week. When a new manager took over an inventory of the contents of the pub was carried out and he was required to sign that it was correct. The inventory for *The Lint* ran to three pages and went into incredible detail. As an example the inventory for Smoke Room number 1 is reproduced on the right. Apparently the only items in the mens lavatory were an electric light fitting, two sheets of obscured glass, a pin rail and five hooks !

The Ladies toilet, however was better off. As well as an electric light fitting, a brass runner and fittings, and a door spring, it also contained a toilet.

In **March 1954** Bill Allison's 14 year old son, Allan hit the local headlines as illustrated below.

There were complaints about the general dilapidation of the premises at this time which led to a inspector's report in **April 1953**.

This report stated that the yard wall was cracked in several places and portions of brickwork might fall into Delagoa Street. The concrete

Smoke Room 1.

1 swing electric light, globe and fittings
4 stools
2 pairs, casement curtains on brass runners
1 domino board, 1 set of dominoes
26 ft of fixed seating and back in rexine
3 circular mahogany topped tables
1 oblong mahogany topped table
1 earthenware spitoon
1 iron curb
1 iron tidy - betty
1 hearthrug
1 framed pricelist
1 fishnet curtains with brass rods and runners
2 framed photographs

Allan, aged 14, has his own museum

SO interested in museums is 14-year-old Allan Allison that over the past two years he has built up his own natural history collection.

Allan — a pupil at Carlisle Grammar School — houses his collection in a room over the Linton Holme Hotel, Lindisfarne Street, which is managed by his father.

The pride of this young curator was obvious when he showed our reporter his museum this week, explaining how he came to accumulate so many exhibits.

He has cases of birds and their eggs, snakes in bottles, and his prize specimen is a handsome red fox—which his mother bought for him in a saleroom.

Most of his specimens have been contributed by friends, while he is himself a keen collector of birds' eggs.

Allan is also a keen painter and has built the cases for the exhibits and designed and executed their settings himself.

Although his main interest is in natural history—particularly bird life—Allan has also accumulated a fearsome collection of weapons from all parts of the

A RED fox is only one of the many exhibits proudly displayed by 14-year-old Allan Allison who has his own museum at his Carlisle home

yard, which had been damaged by a broken water main, had subsequently subsided near the gateway and the wall foundations were in danger. The Off Sales window in Lindisfarne Street was in very bad condition and falling apart. One side of the window had been boarded up and was both untidy and unsafe. Apparently these last faults had been reported three years previously and had since got worse.

In spite of this there is no mention in the records that any of the faults itemised above were ever put right.

However some things were attended to. On **29 March 1954** the Carlisle Superintendent of the State Management Scheme, sent a letter to Mr Stockdale of Binns, Carlisle, regarding curtains which they had supplied some

The Lint in the 50s and 60s. A Darts Alley and a New Bottling Plant at Caldewgate

time previously and which had shrunk in the wash. As a result 'peeping through the windows' was said to be going on. The superintendent wondered if it would be possible to either let down the hem or fit new material to the bottom of the curtains. Binns obliged by adding matching fabric and fitting false hems. Apparently shrinking curtains is still a problem today.

In **October 1954** the State Management Scheme opened its new £96,000 bottling plant at the Caldewgate Brewery, capable of bottling 450 dozen 'bright beers' every hour. This was to cater for the new demand for bright beers without sediment, which were now being produced at Caldewgate. At the same time that the public was demanding beers without sediment, locals at the 'Lint' were putting pressure on 'Mine Host' to provide them

with a '*darts alley.*' Plans were drawn up and the project was costed at £95. This seemed to much for the current financial year and so the plan was postponed until after **April 1955**. By **July 1955** the project was completed and the State Management Inspector reported:

an excellent job and the customers are well satisfied, the only problem is relating to a screen jutting out into the public bar. One has already been removed so the remaining one can be removed, as it serves no useful purpose.

Show cards were displayed in the bar and smoking rooms to indicate the beers on sale and their properties. They are interesting to compare with our present beers (see below right).

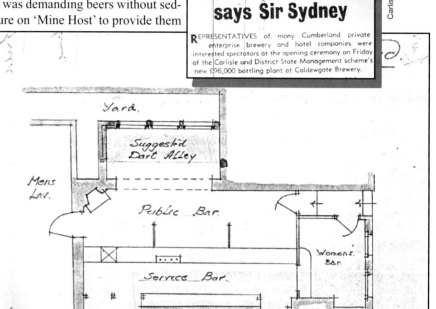

STATE MANAGEMENTS EXTENSION IS OPENED

"Scheme successful" says Sir Sydney

REPRESENTATIVES of many Cumberland private enterprise brewery and hotel companies were interested spectators at the opening ceremony on Friday of the Carlisle and District State Management scheme's new £96,000 bottling plant at Caldewgate Brewery.

Carlisle Journal

Plan of the proposed darts alley

Beers	Bar Price per small bottle	Smoking Room Price per small bottle
Light Ale light in colour and is not a sweet ale, therefore is a dinner ale type of beer	10d	10$\frac{1}{2}$d
Nut Brown Ale High coloured beer, sweet in flavour.	11d	11$\frac{1}{2}$d
Special Beer Similar in nature and character to the present local beer, but at a higher strength.	1/-	1/0$\frac{1}{2}$d
Sweet Stout This stout is smooth to the palate and full drinking and is similar in strength to Special Beer	1/1d	1/1$\frac{1}{2}$d

Reasonable care should be taken in pouring to prevent gushing and too much froth in the glass.

Left: Bottle labels from State Management days   (Ashley Kendall)

87

A Cold Pub, a Missing Stepchair and Eva's Recollections

In December 1961 a 'regular' wrote to the State Management and complained about the cold conditions experienced in the public house: ......*one cannot drink in comfort because it is too cold!*
The State Management reply: ...*many public houses are cold and plans are being considered for improvement to the present heating arrangements, but unfortunately it will take some time before the Linton Holme Hotel has improvements.*

On **8 December 1961** an inventory of hotel furniture found a stepchair to be missing. On querying the whereabouts of the missing stepchair with Bill Allison, the inspector was told that it had been chopped up and used as firewood.
The hotel at this time was heated by coal fires and Eva Douglas, now aged 67, began cleaning in the pub in 1960. Her hours were 9 - 11 a.m. and her tasks included cleaning and setting the coal fires in the rooms. This involved carrying four coal scuttles from the cellar to set the three fires.

Bill and Isabell Allison at Bill's retirement party in 1971

She would scrub the beautiful parquet wooden floors in the rooms, and dust the different size Babychams and the Tucan; which was the Guiness advertisement. She polished the jugs and glasses, including the brass rail along the bar. She also recalls that in those days the main staircase was balusters, not boxed in as it is nowadays. Eva remembers Bill Allison's family well. Allan's interest in collecting and stuffed animals (see page 86) stayed with him into adulthood. He became a museum assistant at Tullie House, where he stuffed animals, eventually becoming a taxidermist in his own right. He is now a wildfowler in Perthshire.
When Les and Mollie Wright took over the pub in 1972 Eva's hours changed so that she worked from 7.30 - 9.30 a.m.. This was because the new manager, Mr Wright, liked her to have her work finished before he came downstairs. Eva does not recall hotel guests as such, but Les and Mollie Wright did have a lot of friends who would

August Bank Holiday mens' outing in on **1 September 1958**. Jimmy Crosbie is circled on the back row. On the second row are circled, right, his father, left, his brother, Jackie Crosbie. The tall man standing behind the group is 'Big Bill' Allison, manager.

visit and stay over. The State Management Scheme was doing quite well in the early 1960s. Bill Monk, the innovative head brewer, produced a prize winning stout, a prize winning nut brown ale and a 'new look' light ale. The fledgling consumer's organisation 'Which' at that time put State Management drink as being *"top value for money."* The Nett profit of the Scheme in 1961 was £178,017 compared with £158,315 the previous year.
Perhaps the increased profits persuaded the Scheme manager to carry out some of the long needed improvements at the 'Lint,' or perhaps it was just responding to tighter health and safety legislation. Whatever the reason in **November 1961** the *"very old fashioned and unsanitary"* urinals were replaced at a cost of £72, and *" in view of the complaints of cold during the previous winter of 1961,"* it was decided, in **October 1962** to install supplementary electric heaters, which it was hoped would *"result in a satisfactory improvement in the comfort of the house."* In **December 1963** an inspector's report stated *"......this house has now been redecorated and some maintenance work is required to finish the job..... The fixed seating in the Smoking Room is dilapidated and needs re-upholstered. The public bar linoleum is shabby and worn out and needs to be renewed."* Accordingly, in **January 1964,** the cost of £75 - 13s. was approved for renovating the fixed seating in two of the smoking rooms. In addition £54 - 7s. was approved to pay for supplying and laying Staines Colourama Super Marble Linoleum in the public bar and the snug. In spite of these improvements, which

Bill Monk, Head Brewer

would be greatly appreciated at the time, the comfort would compare poorly with our modern carpeted and centrally heated pubs. The overall decor was often compared to that of a 'post office.'

1967, the Breathalyser & 1971, the end of State Management

The introduction of the breathalyser in 1967 by Mrs Barbara Castle, the Minister of Transport, was a cause for great concern amongst publicans, particularly those situated in the country.

An original breathalyser, as illustrated in the *Cumberland News*, 8 September 1967.

Licensee Seeks Campaign on Drink - Drive Bill
"The 80mg Farce"

.... the alleged percentage of accidents caused by alcohol is only 6%, the other 94% must be caused by other factors. Drink, like sober incompetence, pressure of commerce, or weather conditions is one of a thousand causes of accidents. The new legislation is ludicrous, most men between 25 and 60 like a drink and are so used to it that it is ludicrous to to regard the 80mg as a universal threat to road safety. .... Frightening people into private drinking and excessive drinking with driving is even more likely..... I ask you to initiate a counter campaign for moderation of the proposed drink driving measures before we are stuck with laws which will accomplish nothing , probably worsen the situation, and bring about a miserable, petty, police state.

Mr J M S Vaux
Landlord,
Haywain,
Little Corby
Chairman of the Brampton Licensed Victuallers Association

Cumberland News, **6 January 1967**

As the date for the introduction of the new test approached publicans looked at ways of alleviating any potential lost business.
29 September 1967
......One landord is making arrangements for a special bus service to be laid on between Carlisle and his country inn, on several days a week. Another is ready to consider a similar scheme if he finds the new laws have an adverse effect on business and a third has had 500 cards printed on *"how not to let the breath test get you down"*...The cards say *"We have got to help ourselves and the police make the best of a thoroughly bad law."*

Cumberland News

Others thought of more ingenius ways of overcoming the problem (below left). The Linton Holme Hotel was probably not adversely affected by the introduction of this law. In fact it may have gained, as fewer people would contemplate driving to a more distant venue and the majority of the Lint's customers lived locally anyway.

On **25 May 1971** a Bill to abolish the State Management Scheme was presented to Parliament. The move was generally welcomed. The *Cumberland News* said:

Good riddance to monopoly. We applaud the death of an experiment which has meant that Carlisle has been discriminated against for over 50 years. The monopoly has held back development and enterprise.

Others were not so sure, as four hundred staff were to be made redundant and many were unsure as to whether they would obtain employment under private ownership. However, Scottish and Newcastle Breweries offered to help some licensees buy their own pubs with loans, giving unlimited time to pay back; on condition they took their beer. Early in 1972 the State Management Scheme began selling off the county pubs. There were 40 pubs in the Carlisle area, to be sold in four groups. Group 1 included the Linton Holme Hotel; which was purchased by William Younger Inns. In **September 1972** relics from the State Management Scheme were auctioned off. Lots of 1000 pewter beer and spirit measures, pewter tankards and earthenware wine and spirit barrels. These were of interest to collectors. Pewter spirit measures were very popular, selling at £1 each.

Pub Transport

GROUP 1 — CARLISLE: Board Inn, Paternoster Row; Border Terrier, Morton; Crescent Inn, Warwick Road; Crown Hotel, Botchergate; Crown, Stanwix; Cumberland Wrestlers, Currock Street; Denton Wine Stores, Denton Street; Globe Inn, Caldewgate; Harraby Inn, Harraby; Joiners Arms, Church Street; Linton Holme Hotel, Lindisfarne Street; Museum Inn, Belle Vue. ABBEY TOWN: Wheatsheaf Inn. ASPATRIA: Sun Inn. CARLETON, Near CARLISLE: Green Bank. DALSTON, Near CARLISLE: Blue Bell. ELLENBOROUGH, MARYPORT: Crown. LITTLE BROUGHTON, COCKERMOUTH: Sun Dial. MARYPORT: Sailors Return. ROCKCLIFFE, Near CARLISLE: Crown and Thistle. SCALEBY, Near CARLISLE:

Licensing (Abolition of State Management)

A
B I L L

To remove the restriction on the sale and supply, otherwise than by the Secretary of State, of intoxicating liquor in the Carlisle district or of exciseable liquor in the State management districts in Scotland; to provide for the disposal of property held by the Secretary of State for the purposes of Part V of the Licensing Act 1964 or Part V of the Licensing (Scotland) Act 1959 and for the repeal of those provisions.

Presented by Mr. Secretary Maudling,
supported by
Mr. Secretary Campbell, Mr. Patrick Jenkin and Mr. Mark Carlisle.

Ordered, by The House of Commons, *to be Printed,* 2 February 1971

LONDON
Printed and Published by
Her Majesty's Stationery Office
Printed in England at St. Stephen's
Parliamentary Press
1s. 6d. [7½p] net

[Bill 100]　　(379824)　　45/1

A Succession of Licensees 1971 - 1984

Les and Mollie Wright previously managed the Irishgate Tavern on Annetwell Street, which was closed in 1971. By the early 1970s inflation had taken its toll and a manager could expect to earn around £16 a week and his wife about £4. Mollie recalls that the 'Lint' was a very busy pub in those days. *"People would come from Botcherby and Harraby to drink at the Lint, where the best beer in town was served."*

Mollie recalls that the 'Lint' was quite dilapidated when they took over. The shop to the right of the pub was boarded up (below). Les and Mollie Wright could not fault the pub or customers, but it was never the same after the State Management ended, so they decide to retire early at the age of 56 years in 1975.

They were followed in **September 1975** by Thomas and Hilda Carr (below left). It was during 'Tommy' Carr's tenancy that structural alterations to the hotel were proposed and granted, although they were never carried out. The alterations involved blocking up the existing hotel entrance and making a new entrance at the top of the cellar steps, facing on to Delagoa Street.

Tragically in **September 1980** Hilda Carr was found dead in the Linton

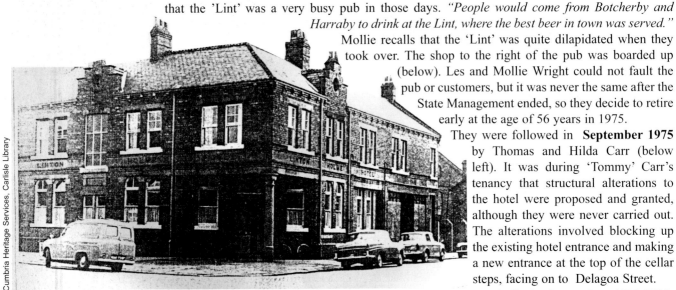
Cumbria Heritage Services, Carlisle Library

Linton Holme Hotel circa 1970

Holme Hotel. The cause of death was 'accidental' as a result of taking quinalbarbitone and alcohol. The following year her husband retired at the age of 58 to a flat in Castle Street. He died two years later of an internal haemorrhage due to Cirrhosis of the liver; an unfortunately common cause of death amongst publicans.

On **15 July 1981** Raymond and Mary Thorburn took over the 'Lint.' Regulars affectionately referred to Raymond as 'T' break. Raymond recalls that the price of a half pint of bitter was $29\frac{1}{2}$p but he would round it up to 30p, as it was easier to count up. They also served bar meals. Ray recalls that the area manager, Chris Hind, asked him to pay £9 per week key money (to cover the cost of electricity etc..). Ray told him he could have his 'key' back! He never had to pay key money after that.

In **April 1982** the pub re-opened after extensive alterations, which includ-ed knocking the individual rooms into one area. Raymond recalls that he wanted to re-open on 1 April as that was his birthday, whereas the building manager, Martin Grant wanted to re-

Hilda and Thomas Edward Carr

open on his birthday (2 April). Raymond remembers that this was the day on which the Falklands War began. At this time they would regularly organise groups to entertain the customers; much to the annoyance of the neighbours. Jimmy Lightfoot, better known as 'Badger' was playing in one of the groups booked. He nailed his big bass drum to the floor through one of the brand new carpets!

They would organise 'Blind Auctions' in aid of the City Maternity Baby Unit, where boxes of all sizes would be wrapped up. No one knew what prize was in the box but would take a chance and bid for them anyway. There was one Friday night when £440 was raised. There was one box, a lot bigger than all the rest and Raymond told the auctioneer to save it til last and his wife, Mary would bid for it. Sure enough she got it. When Mary opened the box she found inside a 'false leg,' belonging to Ted Macafferty; the one legged regular. Everyone was greatly amused.

Raymond in 1997

Raymond and Mary Thorburn in 1982

Joe & Eva, Billy Greer's Football Club and Hamish MacKinnon

Joe and Eva Docherty came to the Linton Holme Hotel in August 1984. It was during their tenancy that

The Young Boys' Football Club was started. Billy Greer ran the football club for 12-14-16 year olds from **1985 to 1992**, using the Linton Holme Public House as a base. He sold 'Spot the Balls' and held discos to raise money to buy their strips. The words ' Linton Holme' were emblazoned on their strip.

In **January 1998** Mrs Greer said: *"A few of the boys still go the the pub today, my son, Michael, Stephen Butcher, David Wallace and Willy, to name but a few."* When the boys reached 16 they could not play in the team anymore, so Billy started the 16 to under 18 years team at Greystone Community Centre. Billy died on **23 April 1992** whilst on a works outing to a football match. He was still selling 'Spot the balls' for the club on the day he died; a mark of his dedication.

One of Billy's boys, Lee Brennan, went on to become famous in his own right with the local band 911.

Joe and Eva Docherty finished at the 'Lint' on **24 March 1986,** leaving Colin Foy, a relief manager, in charge for two months until a replacement was found. Hamish MacKinnon, the new manager, took over in **May 1986**. There were regular live discos at the 'Lint' at this time and they were advertised in the local press (see below).

Joe & Eva Docherty

Billy Greer with John Halpin, now Carlisle United Striker and Coach, receiving the Player of the year Cup in 1985. On the right is Billy's son. Michael Greer.

Below: A line up of junior members of the Linton Holme Football Club.

Above: A Linton Holme Club Squad - Billy Greer is on the right, with his son Mike, front right. Manager Brian Evans is on the left. The player second from the left at the front is a young Lee Brennan of the pop group 911.

Hamish MacKinnon's tenancy of the Lint only lasted 19 months. It was cut short by an unfortunate incident which hit the headlines in the local papers and caused the police to issue a warning for all publicans to be on their guard (see the the next page).

A Mugging, Charity Funding and a Levitation

Shortly after this unfortunate incident Mr MacKinnon vacated his position as manager and on **23 November 1987** a new landlord, George Scott, entered the 'Lint.'

Although he only remained in his post for 9 months, George was presented with a tankard on leaving, in recognition of his good work in sponsoring, through the brewery, the Greystone Football Club.

There now followed a succession of relief managers: Stephen Lord for two months, John Nan Carrow for two and a half months and John James Newbon for seven and a half months.

During this time the regulars and staff at the 'Lint' were doing their bit for charity.

Below: Staff Nurses Josephine Luck and Sally Evans, right, being presented with a cheque for £260 from regulars at the Linton Holme Pub in Carlisle.

The cash, which was raised by barman Michael Jardine, left, and customer Danny Brennan, centre, was collected in a giant whisky bottle which stood in the bar. It was donated to the City Maternity Hospital for the special baby care unit.

George Scott and Tankard

Police Warning to pub landlords

City mugger grabs £1,500

By SIMON REYNOLDS
Crime Reporter

A MUGGER attacked a Carlisle Pub Landlord in broad daylight and robbed him of £1500 sparking a police warning to licensees.

Hamish Mackinnon of the Linton Holme, was grabbed by the neck and dragged to the ground in Linton Street, near London Road., while on his way to a bank.

The attacker snatched a bag full of cash and ran down an alleyway. The incident happened just yards from the pub.

Now police have warned all City landlords to be on their guard, and vary their routine when banking money.

The Linton pub near where the mugger struck

CAREFUL

Mr MacKinnon said: "This bloke came up behind me. It took only two seconds."

"I wasn't hurt, but was upset and shaken up. It seems unbelievable in Carlisle, this sort of thing."

National Westminster Bank PLC

Brian and Brenda Evans

Linty's bottle of good cheer

In **April 1989** Brian and Brenda Evans took up residence in the 'Lint.' A most memorable and unusual event during Brian's stay at the pub was the night he was 'levitated.' by four young ladies. Everyone there was most surprised, not least Brian. According to Marie, the author of this book, he rose up in the air with only minimal support from the helpers.

Right: Brian's levitation caught on camera. Participants Louise, Dorne, Julie and Marie. Nick in the background is just observing.

The Linton Holme Rugby Team

The Linton Holme Rugby Team moved from Chaplins (Cumbria Leisure) in 1989, mainly because Brian and Brenda Evans' son Grant played for the team. John Gibson has been coach for most of the time since the move. The teams most successful season was **1992 - 1993** when they were promoted from the 3rd to the 2nd division as runners up, missing out on the championship on points difference. In the same season they were also runners up in the top four trophy, narrowly losing in the final. In the **1989-91** season Mark Gibson became Players, player-of-the year and man of the match against Accrington. Mark Gibson was also voted top try scorer every year from **1989 to 1994**.

Above: The team before the move to the Linton Holme Hotel

Left: John Gibson, Coach   Above: The team after the move to the Linton Holme Hotel

John Gibson on the Lint Rugby Team
April 1997

In the last couple of years some outstanding players have joined the team.

Steve Preston returned after a couple of years with the Horse and Farrier.. Stuart Herring joined as a teenager and has matured into one of our better players. Marti Nordli joined us from Creighton Rugby Union. Marti is a Canadian married to an Australian. He lives in Scotland and plays for the 'Lint' in England.

Mally Nicholson and Richard McKie were selected for the Cumbria under 19's. Mally played against Great Britain under 19's, but unfortunately Richard had his leg in plaster, due to a rugby injury and was unable to play. In recent years younger players have come to the fore. Lee Manson plays for us in the winter and for Carlisle Border Raiders in the summer. Stuart Herring had never played rugby until he played for us, but in a short time has become and outstanding player. He was put forward for the Great Britain under 23 squad, but was not picked. Mel Heslop joined after playing football for several years, but took to the game right away and is now an individual player. Steve Preston has played since Rugby League first started in Carlisle and is playing some of the best rugby of his life. Mike Bell was a local in the pub before the team moved there but as also become a vital part of the team. He also has played for Border Raiders R.L. David Finlinson has played for several years now, and at the moment travels from Workington to play, where he is manager of the Henry Curwen pub. Tony Winter joined us in his 30's, after an impressive career with Ellenbrough Rangers and Maryport, and is a stalwart in the team. Marti Nordli, who I mentioned earlier, is another reliable player, travelling from Canonbie to play. Craig Marshall and Grant Evans are two of the most competitive players, who the team would miss if they ever stopped playing.

The team has always been competitive and loves to win but they recognise that it is just a game and it is no good getting upset if you lose. The team does well to survive with limited sponsorship. Most of the costs, about £2000 per season, are met by the players themselves. Originally there were 12 teams in and around Carlisle. Now only two remain, the 'Lint' and the St. Nicholas Arms. The surprise of the last few years has been watching Mark Gibson turn from a young player, a painter and decorator, into the manager of a pub (see page 95).

The Early 1990s: Events and Managers

Mark Gibson's achievements on the rugby field were rewarded when he was made captain of the club.

Mark, pictured right of centre in the back row of the adjacent photograph, commented:

" In the last two years I've been made captain, which to me is a real achievement, to captain the team who play from my local pub."

Above: the 1996 team at Workington

On **5 November 1991** Brian and Brenda moved to the Greenbank, Carleton. They were replaced by Ian Thomlinson and Maureen, assisted by Ken Don and Anne. Ken's speciality was his barbecues (see below).

Anne and Maureen

Just 16 months later on **15 February 1993** the hotel changed hands again and Mike Vose became the manager. Only two years later Mike moved on and on **2 February 1995** Brian and Sandra Codonna took over as managers. They had been regulars at the Lint since moving into the area in 1990 and so were already well known to their customers. Brian, a member of the fairground family of Codonnas, had worked part-time as a bar man in the pub for several years. Brian also had the distinction of playing for "Rue and the Rockets" during the late 50s and early 60s and they played in the *Lint* during his managership.

Above: Mike Vose tending to the hanging baskets

Left: **25 April 1995,** the day Carlisle United travelled to Wembley. Mike Bell, a regular for over 20 years, sports his red, white and blue 'Blue Army' haircut

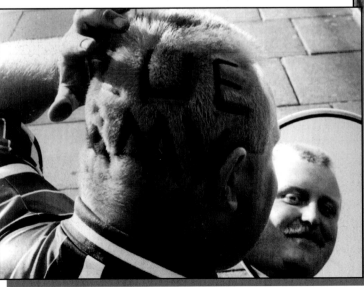

On **8 November 1995** after only a short stay, Brian and Sandra accepted promotion and moved to the 'Prince of Wales' in Denton Holme. They are now managing 'The Cranemakers' and say they miss the

friendly atmosphere of the 'Lint.' They remembered times such as the VE day celebrations in 1995, when Angus brought his motorcycle into the pub.

Brian and Sandra Codonna

Brian and Sandra were succeeded by Mark Gibson, who had been associated with the 'Lint' for eight years, as well as being the star player in the Linton Holme Rugby Team. During his time playing for the Linton Holme Club, Mark had foreseen that he would one day manage the pub. When interviewed he said: *It was always something I'd wanted to do; this place is in my heart. I have had some of the happiest*

Above: Jan, the barmaid at the time, and Sandra (the face).
Left: Mark Gibson, as manager of the 'Lint'

days of my life in the 'Lint,' with the people I had met there. It was just like coming home to one big happy family, having been a regular for eight years.
When asked to recall some of the good times he said that it was hard to pick out any one in particular:
The Kareokes were always good as was the Cup Final event in May 92, when Maureen and Ian organised a fancy dress barbecue.

On **9 April 1997** Mark left the 'Lint' for promotion to 'The Gladstone' in Blackburn (He has since returned to the *Prince of Wales* in Denton Holme).
Just two months before, on **29 January 1997**, Brian Dixon retired as area manager for Scottish and Newcastle. He recalls that he had his first pint of beer as a young man in the Linton Holme Hotel. He began working for S & N in 1983 as wholesale trade territory manager for S & N in the north. Later he went into the training side of the business, and was instrumental in setting up a training college at Chorley.

Brian Dixon

Fancy dress in the beer garden

95

The Linton Holme Football Club (1995 - 97)

Although the 'Lint' sported a football team in the 1950s and 60s, the present team has been playing for two years.

In the 1995/6 season they were Division 2 League champions and League Cup runners up.

In the 1996/7 season they were Division 1 League runners up and League Cup winners.

The Linton Holme Football Club players have an average age of 21years. The team colours are red shirts with navy blue shorts and socks and they play at Melbourne Park.

Right: The 1995/6 team

Alan Bushby and Claire Gartland with their dog 'Deacon' took over as relief managers from **April to June 1997,** when the present manager, Hazel Davis took over, with her dog 'Becks.' Now Hazel's future is uncertain as the *Lint* has been offered on a tenancy from **7 December 1999.**

Page 34 of this book dealt with Percy Dalton, the City Engineer who, in the first half of this century, oversaw the development of the Linton Holme area, as well as much of the rest of Carlisle. It is interesting to note that his descendants still live in the area and his grandson, Angus is a regular customer at the Lint.

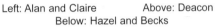

Left: Alan and Claire   Above: Deacon
Below: Hazel and Becks

Angus Dalton, grandson of Percy Dalton, is pictured here with members of his family.

And that brings us just about up to date. In **November 2000** the Linton Holme Hotel will be 100 years old. The original idea for this book was to produce a centenary book for the hotel, just that. When Marie Dickens embarked on this task it quickly developed into something much more. She realised there was a fascinating local history to the area that went back much further than 1899. The hotel was just part of this, providing a social and recreational focus for many of the inhabitants of this developing suburb between Botcherby and London Road.

The result is a detailed social history of the area, enriched with many recollections and images of inhabitants past and present.

All that remains to be said now is:

"Time Ladies and Gentlemen Please"

and thank you for your attention.
We hope that you have enjoyed this book.

Left: Marie Dickens, Author of this book, in the beer garden at the Linton Holme Hotel (1995)